A Journey to Bong Mines

A Journey to Bong Mines

Home Is a Place Best Known to You

Murphy V. S. Anderson

FOREWORD BY
James A. Johnson

RESOURCE *Publications* · Eugene, Oregon

A JOURNEY TO BONG MINES
Home Is a Place Best Known to You

Copyright © 2020 Murphy V. S. Anderson. All rights reserved. Except for brief quotations in critical publications or reviews, no part of this book may be reproduced in any manner without prior written permission from the publisher. Write: Permissions, Wipf and Stock Publishers, 199 W. 8th Ave., Suite 3, Eugene, OR 97401.

Resource Publications
An Imprint of Wipf and Stock Publishers
199 W. 8th Ave., Suite 3
Eugene, OR 97401

www.wipfandstock.com

PAPERBACK ISBN: 978-1-7252-5674-3
HARDCOVER ISBN: 978-1-7252-5675-0
EBOOK ISBN: 978-1-7252-5676-7

Manufactured in the U.S.A.   12/31/19

In loving memory of my late parents,
Murphy K. Sirleaf Sr. and Korto N. Sirleaf

War is the worst act of terrorism and among the greatest causes of human suffering and death and ecological degradation. Wars are declared by the rich and fought by the poor. There will be no real justice and protection of human rights and the rights of nature until a sustainable global peace has been achieved.

—Brian J. Trautman

CONTENTS

Foreword by James A. Johnson | ix
Preface | xi
Acknowledgments | xv
Disclaimer | xvii

1 December 24, 1989 | 3
2 Harbel, Firestone | 7
3 Miracles in the Sunshine | 43
4 The Journey from 45 to Kakata | 61
5 Kakata Police Station | 76
6 Aunt Matenneh's Home | 93
7 The Journey to Bong Mines | 103
8 Bong Mining Company | 116
9 A New Life in Bong Mines | 124
10 Déjà Vu | 138
11 Can't Stop Walking | 145

Appendix: A Glossary of Traditional Liberian
Names and Meanings | 153
Bibliography | 157

FOREWORD

I WAS HAPPY TO be asked by Murphy Anderson to write this short preface for his book *Journey to the Bong Mines*. . . . As his professor, colleague, and friend, I embarked upon reading the manuscript with an open mind. Frankly, I expected to read yet another academic paper, instead what I found was an intriguing and meaningful story, one that like so many of the best stories in history, involves a journey. In this case, a journey based on actual people and events and with many of the elements of the "hero's journey" so famously written about by Joseph Campbell. This involves a hero who goes on an adventure, and in a crisis wins a victory, and then comes home changed or transformed. In the hero's journey much is learned and it is always rich with unanticipated turns, and unexpected outcomes, often better than what could have been imagined. Ultimately, the hero returns home to recognize it for the first time, as if seeing through different eyes.

Murphy's book takes the reader on just such a journey and introduces the world to a part of Africa too often unseen by most. The reader will learn about the fascinating cultural context, social conditions, and human dynamics of this region of the world.

Dr. James A. Johnson, PhD, MPA, MSc,
Professor, Central Michigan University, USA

PREFACE

BEFORE THERE WAS A civil war in Liberia, he always kept in the back of his mind a reason to prepare for the unthinkable, a day when the unimaginable would occur and he must deal with it. Their father usually said to them, "In times of peace, be prepared for war." He'd always tried to figure out the meaning of the statement his father made but failed. He guessed it had to do with the sense of military experiences their father had undergone which always kept reminding him about the need to stay alert and approach life cautiously and circumspectly.

No one knows the future or when the unexpected would occur. Therefore, the inevitability of the unexpected should at least compel us to stay on the alert in preparation for the unthinkable. God has a way of taking us on many journeys in life and creating wonderful opportunities for us to discern his plans toward us. But, because mankind wants to do what he wants and not what God is recommending, we perceive these opportunities as problems and tend to use our human ingenuity to solve them. Also, because mankind refuses to remain a thinking creature and think through situations, negative or positive, we are likely to blame others or seek to take the so-called "easy way out." The predictable outcomes of our actions, as we know, are not always in our best interest. Fortunately, God never gives up on us; he stays with us through it all.

This is a true story about four boys who had journeyed back to their hometown, a place they considered the safest in a country torn by civil war caused by tribalism, nepotism, sectionalism, greed for power, corruption, and abuse of authority, disregard for human dignity, and bigotry. Though the boys were familiar with the terrain in Bong Mines, they miscalculated and overlooked the dangers and all the maneuverings they had to go through to survive in a civil war and reach home safely. They did not think the journey home would have been so hard and fearful that the safety of

xi

PREFACE

their lives would have most likely depended on the miracles of God and the shoulders and ingenuity of Kerkula, their older brother.

Often we take God for granted, but he remains faithful to his word. His goodness and mercy endure forever. His grace pours down always toward us like rainfall when we least expect it. He is not a man that he should lie, neither a son of man that he may commit sin. His plan toward us is meant to prosper us and not to harm us. He will never leave us nor forsake us, and he will never allow us to go through situations alone but will always find a way of escape for us (1 Cor 10:13 NIV).

In his wisdom and purpose, God brought Kerkula to Harbel in a time and moment when his parents, brothers, and sisters would need him the most. Plunged into the heat of the civil crisis, his parents were dumbfounded and underestimated the magnitude of what was happening before their eyes and what was yet to come. Little did he know that eventually the unexpected was about to engulf his peaceful community like the rising tides of the Atlantic Ocean or the sweeping strength of a mighty tornado. All that his father had warned and cautioned him and his siblings about would come so quickly, as though it was a prophecy handed down from the heavens to them.

He assumed an unimaginable responsibility of his family and saved their lives by taking five appropriate steps. First, he depended on God for guidance to lead his parents and siblings out of harm's way. Second, he made sound and timely decisions. For example, he asked his parents and siblings to leave the house in Harbel before the rebels got to it and immediately changed the last names of everyone from Sirleaf to Kerkula, since the name Sirleaf was somewhat associated with the Mandingo tribe; one of the tribes that was being hunted by the first group of rebels. Third, he strategically separated his family into groups of three (males, females, and their father) and gave them two instructions; stay safe and head to Bong Mines if possible. The fourth step was he made sure that no one was left behind but that everyone reached the place called home. It took them almost a month to travel on foot from Harbel, Firestone, to Botota, Bong Mines.

The stories discussed in this book are true about the individuals who revealed them to the writer. The revelations contained herein are in no ways meant to relive the memories of events that transpired in the lives of these four boys or their family. Neither are they intended to decry, ridicule, or demonize anyone else. The names mentioned are real and the events

xii

PREFACE

occurred. For the most part, this story is true to the author's recollections even though it has been several years since the actual events occurred.

The primary purpose of this book is to fulfill the following: (1) Serve as a testimony about the unwavering goodness and love of God especially in crisis or when all seems to go wrong; (2) Reveal the power of God in performing miracles when darkness seems to prevail; (3) Tell the story of how God saved the lives of four young boys but especially used one of them immeasurably to guide and lead the rest of his family to safety.

ACKNOWLEDGMENTS

THE COMPLETION OF THIS book would have been absolutely and unequivocally impossible if it hadn't been for love, trust, support, and prayers from the following individuals who I would like to thank in this public manner: Mr. Murphy K. Sirleaf Sr., my father, for his love, trust, and gift of life; Korto N. Sirleaf, my mother for giving me life and care; Betty Schaffer, and Ruth G. Jackson, for their unwavering motherly love, support, and care; Mr. Varney M. Feemorlu, for his spiritual guidance and love; Mr. Alfred Davies, for his help and support; Rev. G. Nathaniel B. Garpu, BTh, for his steadfast leadership; Mr Joseph D. Kennedy, BA, for his resourcefulness and brotherhood; Dr. Joseph W. Smith, MD, for his resourcefulness and friendship; and everyone who I spoke with in gathering information from Liberia.

A special thanks to Dr. James A. Johnson for writing the preface; Mrs. Mydea-Reeves karpeh and Mrs. Chelahnne Lyons for their assistance with editing the manuscript; Mr. Bill N. Sirleaf, my younger brother, for his assistance in gathering accurate information provided in this book, including current pictures about Bong Mines, traditional names and meanings, people, events, and places. Thank you!

DISCLAIMER

LIMIT OF LIABILITY / DISCLAIMER OF Warranty: The author has used his best judgments and efforts in preparing this book. Therefore, he makes no representations or warranties with respect to the accuracy or completeness of the content of this book. He specifically disclaims any implied warranties of merchantability or fitness for a particular purpose. No warranty may be created or extended by sales representatives or written sales materials. The strategies used by the characters in this book may not be suitable or applicable in your situation. Therefore, the author shall not be liable for damages arising herefrom. The author does not necessarily endorse any organization or website because of the information gathered from them and/or cited in this book. The author wishes to caution his readers to be aware that some of the websites cited may have been removed, changed, replaced, or no longer exist between when this book was written and when it was finally published.

Part One

CHAPTER ONE

December 24, 1989

HE NEVER THOUGHT GOING back to his hometown, the village where his grandparents were born, would have been so compelling to him or his siblings until the unthinkable happened. Sometimes, life judges or surprises us beyond our wildest imagination and dreams, especially when the unexpected happens. This was the experience of Kerkula and his three brothers. He did not know or expect the danger that was coming their way until it hit them surprisingly on an early sunny morning in February 1999. Before leaving Gbarnga, the news and activities of a rebel invasion in the northern part of Liberia had been announced both on the national and local radio stations. The rebel incursion started on December 24, 1989. It forced Kerkula to flee their home in Gbarnga and took refuge with his parents in Harbel. He had to leave Gbarnga quickly because the rebels' activity was intensifying too rapidly, and there was not enough time to waste.

As usual, the market in Harbel seemed crowded with customers and local merchants who often came from the nearby towns and villages. Some came from a small town with an unusual name, Smell-No-Taste, while others came from Monrovia and other cities far and near to transact business and conduct other personal activities. Smell-No-Taste is located a few miles off Robert Field Highway by way of Monrovia, the capital city of Liberia. One would have to drive off the main highway for a few miles before entering the town. There were and still are today many rationales behind the name Smell-No-Taste. As practical as the name sounds, one would think the name has no importance to be placed on a town. One may think that the name is a joke. Some Liberians believe that the city was named Smell-No-Taste due to the stingy, closed-fisted, and parsimonious behaviors of the "Bassa tribe" who were the first predominant settlers in the area. Other Liberians are convinced the erratic behaviors of other inhabitants living

3

in the city may have been the reason behind the name. No matter how the city received its name, it has left an indelible imprint on its inhabitants, especially to the older generation.

An elderly gentleman whom I spoke with described how the city received its name. He said, "The early Bassa tribal group living in the Smell-No-Taste area was naturally and undeniably parsimonious. The tribe would cook delicious meals and the sweet-smelling aroma which burst into the atmosphere would attract visitors and residents from other communities." However, when a member of the tribe was asked to share some of his or her food with others, his or her reply was usually predictable and not surprising. Nevertheless, visitors continued to ask members of the tribal group to share meals with them. A member of the tribe would always say, "I have no food and have not cooked all day for my family to eat." Sooner or later, it became noticed as an everyday cry particularly from the Bassa inhabitants when it came to share meals with others in the community.

Notice, the emphasis for which the town was named, Smell-No-Taste, was mainly due to the Bassa tribal group's refusal to share their meals with others. It was not necessarily because the tribe did not share any other possessions or belongings with others as has been suggested by some. Even though the Bassa tribe was notorious for being stingy and unwilling to share anything and everything with their neighbors, it led some residents to believe because of such attitude, the name Smell-No-Taste was suddenly born. The irony was as stingy as the Bassa inhabitants were about sharing cooked meals with visitors and other residents, they cultivated a constant habit of asking others within the area for ingredients like Maggi cubes, pepper, sesame seeds (bene seeds), firewood, pots, and other cooking utensils that they used to cook. To this day, the elderly gentleman doesn't know any other reasons behind the name other than the reasons previously discussed. No one else has told him a different version of exactly why residents of Smell-No-Taste gave the community such a name.

Back in the days, Smell-No-Taste was one of several known local communities in Marshall which flourished and was inhabited by Liberians who came from different parts of the country. Some residents who lived in Smell-No-Taste worked, transacted businesses, and went to church and school in Harbel (a.k.a. Division 45). This is one reason why the community was popular or seemed to generate lots of attention from market-goers, merchants, and visitors who came to the town to transact business or to conduct other personal engagements. There are Liberians who believe that Smell-No-Taste

DECEMBER 24, 1989

gained its prominence among the colony of local communities in Liberia primarily because of how simple and casual the name sounded. It is unfortunate that there are other Liberians who hold onto the beliefs and stigmatize residents of this community as being self-centered and egotistic. Whatever the belief was or is now about residents of Smell-No-Taste, one fact is true: they loved to come to the market in Harbel, especially on payday weekends or what we call in Liberia, "Market Day."

The drive to Smell-No-Taste before heading to Harbel was short. Kerkula and his driver did not have the opportunity to see and interact with the locals as much as they had hoped. He had learned about this community growing up and how its residents usually behaved to strangers, which made him interested in verifying the informed for himself. Instead of taking another route to get to Harbel, he'd thought the time was right to travel to the city to gather some information about its residents, especially in such a time when the country was on the brink of a civil war. He believed, if anyone was to show hospitality to another person, this was the appropriate time to do so. Kerkula realized they had come closer to Harbel, their final destination, and there was no need to rush home. He was convinced they'd finally escaped the danger of the rebels' invasion, and there was no need to panic. He had quickly forgotten all that he and his driver had gone through, leaving Gbarnga to get this far.

As they drove through town, there were people walking the streets talking and transacting business while others were standing in smaller groups along the way as though it was market day. He rolled down his window, stuck his head out, and whispered to an older gentleman sitting on a bamboo chair, sipping palm wine and smoking tobacco through a wooden pipe. Palm wine/bamboo wine is a locally produced alcoholic beverage made from palm trees and sold in the local markets. It is usually consumed by the locals, especially men.

"What is going on around here that there are people everywhere?" Kerkula asked the older gentleman. "Is today market day, and has the market day changed?" Kerkula continued with his questions.

"No, my son! It is not market day; the day has not changed!" the elderly man replied.

"Well, we heard there are strange people with guns and other weapons coming our way from the northern border."

A JOURNEY TO BONG MINES

"Everyone is afraid and has come out of their individual homes as quickly as possible to get food items and other household supplies before the war reaches this area," the old man said reluctantly.

"We saw lots of people along the way on our drive here. They seemed to have come from the same direction you are talking about," Kerkula added. "Do you know where we can purchase some cooked food to eat?" Kerkula asked the older adult.

Kerkula tried to change the discussion between him and the older man by asking different questions. He wanted to make sure that he felt comfortable talking with him. Throughout their interaction, Kerkula kept his eyes directly toward the old man but slightly away from his face. Traditionally in African cultures, especially in Liberia, it is a sign of disrespect for a younger person to look an elder face-to-face while talking to him or her. Kerkula knew this well and dared not disobey. He continued his talk with the elderly man.

"We have been driving all day and are feeling hungry," Kerkula said.

The elderly man smiled, shook his head and looked away.

"Where are you coming from, and where are you going?" The old man asked.

"We are from Gbarnga and headed to Harbel," Kerkula replied!

"Walk down this road and go behind the third hut next to that grapefruit trees, pointing his finger to what seemed like fruit trees with many fruits on them. Go to the second house after the fruit trees, and you will find a woman who has a cook shop (a.k.a., restaurant)."

The older gentleman politely gathered his bamboo chair and walked away. He may have figured that Kerkula and his driver were up to no good, and he did not want to be bothered any longer. Disappointed by the older man's reaction, Kerkula decided they would go directly to Harbel instead of finding food as previously desired. It was the only opportunity he had to experience hospitality in Smell-No-Taste before the war reached Harbel, but he failed to utilize it.

6

CHAPTER TWO

Harbel, Firestone

HARBEL, FOR THE MOST part, had always been a peaceful place to live. The city was mostly quiet and friendly. "Division 45" as it was affectionately called or interchangeably used was mostly sunny and breezy. The smooth soothing breeze from the Atlantic Ocean in the southern part of the country was felt during the day but mostly during the early hours of the evening. It made evening hours more beautiful to take walks around the neighborhood, sit on the lawn or walk under the night lights. Back then, kids and their parents would come out on the soccer field, right in the heart of town, to watch movies on a big screen which was projected on the walls of the administrative building. They would sit on the lawns in the night lights and watch movies all night till midnight. It was obvious that many times, moviegoers would forget that it was midnight and time to go home because the atmosphere was peaceful, and everyone seemed friendly. Moreover, the constant and available presence of the Plant Protection Department (PPD) security guards made the community even more safe and dependable for residents and visitors alike. Most times, one could literally walk through town or in the surrounding neighborhoods and feel a sense of safety and protection just by the presence of the PPD guards.

Though Harbel was a peaceful city, it remained mostly busy. By busy, I mean, the city was constantly attracting new residents and visitors from other cities around the country. Harbel is about thirty miles east of Monrovia, along the Camp Schieffelin-Robert's Field Highway. By contrast, it was the seat of authority, which accommodated the Central Office, senior management offices, and other working facilities for Firestone Rubber Plantation Company, one of Africa's oldest Rubber Plantation Companies. Historically, in 1926, Firestone and the government of Liberia signed a concessional agreement during the leadership of Charles D. B. King, seventeenth president of the Republic of Liberia, and Harvey Firestone, president and founder of the Firestone Natural Rubber Plantation Company.

Driven by his ambition to make America self-reliant and independent in the production of natural rubber after World War I, Harvey Firestone engaged the government and people of the Republic of Liberia for the use of their land to produce natural rubber. He became troubled when the price of rubber on the international market dropped sharply and the government of the United Kingdom, which dominated and monopolized rubber production around the world, swiftly introduced measures intended to control the supply of rubber on the world market. Amid protest from residents and international organizations doing business in Liberia at the time, the concession was subsequently agreed upon and signed, giving Firestone the exclusive rights and authority to begin the production of natural rubber for ninety-nine years on the soil of Liberia. Since the signing of the original contract between the government of Liberia and Firestone, there have been some renegotiations of the contract by recent presidents over the past ten years with considerations made to specific sections but not entirely. However, the terms and agreements of the contract have remained mostly the same, with Firestone being the largest rubber-producing company in Liberia, and Africa at large.

On March 18, 2019, a story carried in *FrontPage Africa* reported that Firestone planned to lay off eight hundred employees, about 13 percent of its workforce, beginning in the early quarter of 2019. The move by Firestone was expected to encourage or force early retirements of some employees who have probably reached the required age. The move was also intended to allow the company to review and possibly discontinue unproductive work contracts and to eliminate areas of redundancies within their operations. It was believed that the company's decision to reposition its operations came as a result of a decrease in the price of rubber globally, financial losses sustained from inadequate production and exportation of rubber during the civil war, and the prohibitive costs of doing business, including overhead.

In the wake of those changes, employees along with their families were concerned about their future with the company and the livelihoods of their children. It was not made known if the management of Firestone intended to recommend more future layoffs or would continue its operations in Liberia at an increased capacity to create reemployment opportunities in the future for laid-off workers. We can only hope that the price of rubber on the global market would begin to rise again so that Firestone is in the position to create more employment opportunities for Liberians and put them back into the workforce to support and sustain themselves and their families.

Based on the current global market activities of rubber, it is projected that global consumption of rubber will slow down in 2019 because of expected lower global economic growth, concerns and geographic issues, and trade war. Additionally, emerging economic trends, the value of the dollar and an increase in the price of crude oil are also adversely impacting the decrease in the price of rubber. However, according to Jom Jacob, senior economist for the Association of Natural Rubber Producing Countries (ANPRC), rubber consumption is expected to increase at a slower rate of 4.2 percent to 14.590 million ton in 2019 compared to the 5.2 percent rate of growth preliminary estimated for 2018.

Hopefully, a shift in the price and consumption of rubber on the global market will begin to increase as suggested by Jom Jacob. This may help boost Firestone's exportation of rubber and subsequently pave the way to rehire more workers.

A Visit to "Division 45"

He had gone to Harbel almost at the end of December 1989 after the news of a rebel invasion into a Northern Liberian town of Luagatou in Nimba County was announced on the national radio and on the British Broadcasting Corporation *Focus on Africa* program. The rebels who called themselves "Freedom Fighters" were led by Mr. Charles Taylor and the National Patriotic Front of Liberia (NPFL). Mr. Taylor and the NPFL claimed that the primary purpose of their fight was to overthrow the democratically elected government of President Samuel K. Doe and the National Democratic Party of Liberia (NDPL) on accusations of rampant corruption, tribalism, injustices, and the misuse of Liberia's natural resources.

His trip to "Division 45" was at the invitation of his father who had asked him to come down so he could help his little brothers and cousin to shop for Christmas gifts, household supplies, and to talk about plans on moving the family from Gbarnga to Mahwah, their hometown, in the event the incursion reached them. Before his trip to "Division 45," the news about the rebels' activities had partly subsided. At least there was no active news for a while. However, the evidence suggested that the magnitude of the incursion needed not to be taken lightly. There were movements of large numbers of displaced people in trucks, cars, and on foot from the bordering towns in Nimba County. There was also a mustering of government troops to the border, and wounded soldiers and civilians from battlegrounds or front lines were being transported in ordinary commercial and often, military-controlled vehicles. At the time, some Liberians who had not experienced the hostilities or weren't knowledgeable about rebel warfare thought the entire incursion was a hoax. They prematurely decided to stay in their respective localities, did not take further precautions to protect themselves from the coming danger.

The news about the rebels' movements began to subside even much more than expected. There was news circulating in Gbarnga that government troops had dismantled and flushed the rebel resistance out of Nimba County and was in full control of the county. Little did Kerkula and other Liberians know that militarily, a retreat of rebel troops or fighters doesn't necessarily mean a defeat. Instead, it could be a strategy to regroup and return on an aggressive attack. Publius Cornelius Tacitus, a senator and historian of the Roman Empire, once said, "He that fights and runs away, may turn and fight another day; but he that is in battle slain will never rise to fight again." This seemed to have been the tactics of the rebels. Unfortunately, some Liberians and even the Armed Forces of Liberia (AFL) failed to recognize these tactics by the rebels or may have recognized them but were overwhelmed and didn't take the necessary steps quickly to avoid human causalities, especially the innocent civilians.

The shortage of taxi cabs plying the streets due to the news of the incursion made it difficult for Kerkula to find reliable public transportation for his trip to Harbel. Worse of all, taxi drivers had inflated the price of transportation from Gbarnga to other parts of the country blaming the hike on the shortage of gasoline. There were few public transport vehicles going toward the incursion areas. Drivers who were brave to travel a route toward the bordering towns where the incursion started charged a prodigious amount per passenger. In fact, they charged even more astronomically for a chartered service. A chartered service is the transporting of cargo or people who have contracted to have exclusive use of a vehicle, aircraft, or vessel at a fixed rate, under one contract, for a specified location, and for a field trip.

He tried a couple of times, day after day to find a taxi going directly to Harbel but his efforts failed. He even tried to find a vehicle that was going to Kakata, a town in route to Harbel which is approximately forty-five minutes to an hour drive depending on the route you take and how fast you were driving but no one was available. All the taxis that were headed in that direction were either already booked or very expensive. Fortunately, an elderly gentleman who lived in the nearby community was contacted and he agreed to rent his car. All arrangements for the use of the car, a Peugeot 504, were made under a chartered service agreement between Kerkula and the owner; the trip to Harbel was finalized and a date was set.

Brooklyn—Rubber Factory—Police Station

On the morning of the trip to Harbel, the streets of Gbarnga were crowded with more displaced people coming from Nimba County and headed to Monrovia. Some of the displaced said they were only taking precaution by relocating to other cities where life was normal, while others made it emphatically clear, asking people to find a safe place to go because the rebels were murdering innocent people indiscriminately.

Early the next morning, the driver arrived, and they began to load the 504 for the trip to Harbel. There were people who had asked Kerkula for a ride in his chartered car, but he could not take anyone. The car was full and had no additional space to accommodate another person. Moreover, fulfilling one person's request for a ride would absolutely mean fulfilling all requests or be considered partial and selfish if one request was considered above the others in such a desperate situation.

At approximately 11:45 a.m., the driver stepped on the clutch, shifted gears, and slowly but surely pressed his foot on the accelerator as the car began to roll out of the driveway onto the local street that passes before their yard. That was the last time he laid his eyes on what he once called home. It was the first time in many years that a sense of fear and urgency gripped and overcame him, shattering his confidence into complete dejection. His world collapsed momentarily as the 504 turned the corner and the reflections of the yellow and brown paint on his father's home quickly disappeared from his sight. He struggled initially to understand why so much chaos had erupted so abruptly in Liberia that innocent people were being forced to leave their homes and settle in unknown destinations. His mind failed to rationalize the reasons for warfare and destruction of properties even at the peril of other people's lives.

Throughout their early drive from the community, he became increasingly troubled as they drove through the neighborhoods where he once spent time with his friends. He'd feared that some of his friends he was leaving behind were not in the position to escape the coming danger or were not taking the rebels' advancement toward the city of Gbarnga seriously, even though the evidence were clearly visible and factual. He could not imagine why rational people could become so dumbfounded and oblivious to reality as though they were mentally incapacitated.

A couple of minutes into the final drive from the community, the car stopped abruptly at the traffic sign next to the police station in Brooklyn just before making a left turn onto the main paved road that leads southbound out of the city toward Kakata. There were many people standing outside the walls of the police station. He was not sure why some people were standing while others were seated on the ground. There were policemen fully dressed up in their police gear and a couple of men in handcuffs on the ground.

The movement of police and civilians in and out of the police station was quick and unprotected as though it was a marketplace and not a police station. Brooklyn, or Rubber Factory, Police Station, as it was often interchangeably called, was known for its quiet and professional environment and activities. Whenever you went to this police station to visit, one could sense a uniqueness of law and order. There was a certain prestige about this police station unlike some other police stations around the country. The police officers back then were dignified, professional, well dressed, and law abiding. This is in no way suggesting that the current police department in Gbarnga does not possess these unique qualities. History will bear us witness that time has changed and continues to change. The police and paramilitary officers we once knew in Gbarnga for the level of professionalism, duty to protect country, and citizens, interpersonal skills, and sound discipline are somewhat or totally different from what we see today. Again, this is not meant to decry the current law enforcement departments in our county or city. We recognize and honor the incredible sacrifices they are making in the city of Gbarnga and Bong County. We also applaud them for all that they do. However, history will judge us if we fail to acknowledge and give honor also to those who came before them.

He rolled down his window to catch a clear glimpse of the people standing in the distance at the police station. His eyes became weary as he moved them left to right trying to identify anyone in the crowd that he knew. He also looked at those sitting down on the ground, along the street sidewalks, and at those who went up to the station but didn't recognize anyone. The driver began to turn left on the paved road; hence, he decided to roll his window back up, since he did not recognize anyone, and they were about to leave. Suddenly, he heard a sharp knock on the trunk of the 504 and someone shouted his name, "Kerkula! Kerkula!" It scared him and his chartered driver. Frantically, the driver quavered but managed to pull the car to the side of the road. As he tried to turn his head around and see what had happened, he heard another knock, this time on the back window from the passenger's side where he was seated. He lifted his head quickly, and soon a skinny tall image appeared before him on the window of the car. A hand signaled him to roll down his window.

Hesitantly, he began to roll down his window. At first, he thought the driver had committed a traffic violation, but spun disdainfully, saying, um, it can't be true! "Maybe, someone wants our help," he said quietly to the driver as though he did not want the person standing outside the car to hear him. Gradually, he rolled down his window and soon realized that what had surprised them, needed no surprise. He came face-to-face with the tall skinny image as he fully appeared and showed his face.

"Kerkula! Kerkula! Thank God it is really you, man!" he exclaimed. "Where are you going in this car so packed? Are you running away from town? Are you leaving us here? Please, can you take me to Monrovia? I would like to go to Paynesville and stay at my oldest brother's house? This is becoming too much scary and I cannot take it anymore," the friend said.

"Frankie, is that you?" Kerkula asked. "Oh man! I never thought I would have seen you before leaving town," Kerkula exclaimed. "I am so glad that I have seen you," said Kerkula. He looked at his friend with excitement in his voice and a smile on his face.

He straightened up the car seat, pushed the door opened and stepped out. He gave his friend a tight bear hug and muttered, "Hopefully not for the last time. No one knows what is going to happen in the next couple of months with all of this chaos. Let's hope that I can see you again. The car is full and there is no empty seat to take you along," Kerkula lamented.

"I was just kidding, Kerkula," Frankie replied boldly. "I am not going anywhere; I am not leaving this city. I was born here and will die here. If anyone wants to drive me away from this place which I call home, let them be my guest," Frankie said audaciously. Frankie became vehemently vociferous and hypersensitive as he spoke about the rebel's activities and his willingness to stand his ground against anyone who attempted to drive him out of town, as though he and Kerkula were in a debate. They bade each other goodbye and promised to take loving care until they met again.

A JOURNEY TO BONG MINES

Years ago, during their teenage days, Frankie and Kerkula became good friends after they met at a basketball practice on a high school campus. Before they were good friends, they were rivals. There is an adage which says, "The tongue and teeth live under the same roof but yet they seem to fight each other every time." Frankie attended a private high school and Kerkula went to a public high school. During their high school days, there was a stigma about kids who went to public schools. It was often thought by some, especially the fortunate Liberians or upper class, that parents who sent their kids to public schools were either poor or considered "country or native people." On the contrary, parents who sent their kids to private schools were considered "rich or Congo People," also referred to as "Americo-Liberians."

The "Congo People" in Liberia are the descendants of freed African slaves from America and the Caribbean who became settled in Liberia in 1822 after gaining their freedom from their slave masters. Frankie was a "Congo Boy" and had lots of friends because his parents were rich, and he could afford to share his lunch and other goodies with his playmates at school. Girls liked him for what he could give them, or they could get from him and not necessarily who he was. He was not one of the cutest boys. Occasionally, he was argumentative, vociferous, and braggadocios about his parents' wealth. He knew his sense of bigotry attracted some un-level-headed, gravy-seeking friends. Equally, his bigotry and annoyance repelled those friends and girls who knew their individual identities and reasons for their friendship with him. Interestingly, he was not one of the brightest minds among his peers.

On the other hand, Kerkula was smart and polite. He was the second son of his parents. In fact, if we consider the number of kids his parents had who did not survive prior to giving birth to him; he would have been the fourth kid in line, born unto the union of his parents. He and his family were originally from the Kpelle tribe and originated from Mahwah, a small tribal town along the St. Paul River in Fumah District, lower Bong County, Liberia. The Kpelle tribe is one of sixteen tribal groups in Liberia. His father was a commissioned officer in the AFL and held the rank of first lieutenant and deputy commanding officer of the Fifth Infantry Battalion in Gbarnga, Bong County, prior to the civil war. He served in this position for a couple of years before his promotion to the rank of captain and elevated to the position as deputy regional commander for Bong, Nimba, and Lofa Counties, respectively.

14

HARBEL, FIRESTONE

During the 1970s and 1980s, a captain did not earn much monthly income to support a large family of eight. Kerkula's parents were not financially able to send all their children to private schools. Moreover, it would have been unfair to send some of the children to private schools while the others went to public schools. The public school system in Liberia during the 1970s and 1980s was not as bad as it is today, neither was it as good as other African or European countries. Nevertheless, the educational system was unique and provided a level of education that Liberians were comfortable with and appreciated.

Public schools were not adequately funded by the government compared to the level of financial and logistic support the private institutions received. Students in private schools like Frankie could always brag about the standard of their schools and the benefits they enjoyed. Unlike private school students, there was not much public-school kids could boast about collectively other than bragging about individual success and academic achievements. Kerkula attended all public schools throughout his high school years. He was privileged to attend private school once as a student in seventh grade at Anna F. Wilson Elementary and junior high school in Sanniquellie, Nimba County, during the reign of the People's Redemption Council (PRC) government.

The divide in educational opportunities that existed in both the public and private school sectors troubled Kerkula sometimes but more especially when he interacted with Frankie and his other friends. He became critical of why public schools were not as good as private schools and why wouldn't the government spend more on education when it is the sole foundation for the successful development of any nation. He later came to find out after he left high school and grew much older that systems (e.g., educational system) are built by wise people but can become corrupted and mismanaged when left in the hands of the wrong people or government.

His mother was a typical native woman from a small village called Kpakoquayata (Kpa-ko-qua-ya ta) in Bong County. His father met his mother in the early sixties when he attended the Booker Washington Institute (BWI) in Kakata, Margibi County, where he became a student in the auto mechanic department. As it was typical for some women in Liberia years ago, his mother did not attend school; she decided to remain a "stay-home mom" and chose a career in becoming a local merchant, selling local produce in the public market, a term that is usually referred to in Liberia as "market woman." She could hardly read or write but was highly industrious and innovative. She had a good sense of commerce and could conduct elevated levels of business transactions with fewer or no mistakes made. Friends in the marketplace knew her very well because of her sound mind and good judgments. Though she was not formally educated, they depended on her for guidance, even those that had some level of formal education.

The monthly proceeds Kerkula's mom generated from merchandise sales were used to supplement for school materials that her kids needed and to assist her husband, Kerkula's father, with his tuition at BWI. His father always referred to her as the "backbone of the family." Her friends called her "the ever-smiling but never-failing woman." Those who knew and interacted with her praised her for the life she lived. She was quiet, pretty, and warm in her interactions with all who crossed her path. She intentionally sought out to do good as she was able and had the strength and ability to do. No one compares to her! She was affectionately called *Nay Korto*, meaning "mother Korto" in Kpelle. She will forever be missed.

Kerkula was one of his parents' prides. He was terrifically smart growing up and had an exquisite appearance and attitude about him. His friends loved him because of his gifted mind, irresistible smile, and friendship. He smiled constantly as though he never had a difficult day or his mind preoccupied. His friends always wondered if he ever became upset or angry. Unlike his friend Frankie, not many girls liked him. Probably because he did not have goodies to offer them or lunch to share as Frankie did. Nevertheless, apart from his brilliant mind, he had other talents. Kerkula played both basketball and volleyball well and his friends loved him for that. For some odd reason, his ability to play both sports well attracted several girls to him. Some of the girls who thought Kerkula was admirable were often noticed hanging out with Frankie's group of girls. Interestingly, this is how the rivalry started between both.

Whenever Kerkula went to play basketball or volleyball on the court, his friends literally scrambled among themselves to have him play on their team. He was that good at the level of his game and he knew it. He also had a gift of writing. He discovered that he had a gift of writing when he began to write short poems and recitations during his teenage years without anyone couching or mentoring him. Apparently, the gift of writing is hereditary. Kerkula's dad was just the same way. His dad literally wrote down any and every idea that flowed through his mind when he was alive. It was interesting how on many occasions his dad would take a note pad or what we call "writing pad" in Liberia and sit by the radio to listen to *Focus on Africa*, a British Broadcasting Corporation (BBC) news service that focuses mostly on current events happening in Africa. *Focus on Africa* news program is a portion of BBC World News and airs at 15000, 17000, and 19000 Greenwich Mean Time (GMT), respectively, on Monday to Friday, and 1900 GMT on Saturday and Sunday. The BBC news program is an informative and educational news outlet that broadcasts in thirty-nine languages worldwide.

Kerkula's dad was a faithful listener of the *Focus on Africa* news program. He would spend hours listening to the news and other updates and would jot down every major point on the news and would turn those points into a diary. His dad would then find time to make sure that he discussed those major points with some of his kids or his friends in the neighborhood. Mr. Teeer, his next-door neighbor, was one of the many friends that his dad held conversations with regularly. Both his dad and Mr. Teekeh were good buddies and wore the uniform of AFL together as commissioned officers. In fact, Mr. Teekeh held the same rank of 1st Lieutenant that Kerkula's father held long before he rose to the rank of Captain. Also, they were both men of the same tribal society and had several traditional, cultural practices and norms in common that they respected and honored. Both men ended up retiring from the AFL in the same year and continued as friends until the untimely death of Kerkula's father on May 1, 2013.

He clearly remembers up to this day what really transpired between him and Frankie that resulted in a rivalry they had between them before becoming good friends. It all started one evening; he'd gone to play basketball at the same basketball court where they always gathered. There were other teenage boys who had come to practice. Some of the boys came with their girlfriends and others didn't. Frankie had not come for practice when Kerkula arrived. Usually, practices were held during the late afternoon after the high school afternoon study classes were out of session. It was being done this way to give the students privacy and avoid loud noises, which tend to disturb them during study classes. Boys standing around the basketball court did not have a ball to play with. Hence, they waited for anyone who would have brought one. Kerkula arrived shortly after the afternoon classes were over.

As he and his friend walked between the school buildings, his name echoed against the walls. "Kerkula! . . . Kerkula! . . . Kerkula! Come and play on my team. Do you have a ball?" the voice shouted.

He looked in the distance to take a glimpse at the caller but failed to recognize who exactly was calling his name because there were too many people. As he came closer toward the basketball court, an old-time friend that he usually played volleyball with jumped out of the crowd of teenagers and ran toward him excitingly and shook his hand.

"I am glad that you made it to practice today. For some reason, I was skeptical of you coming to practice because your old man did not go to work today. Usually, he wouldn't have allowed you to come out to practice had he seen you," Stone said.

"Why you would say that and how do you know all of this," Kerkula asked. "You seem to know too much about me, more than I know about myself," Kerkula continued. "I am here to play and that's all that matters!" Kerkula added with a smile on his face.

Both boys shook hands, pulled each other back and forth like two dogs playing. They finally settled down and headed onto the court to play basketball.

"Where is the basketball?" Kerkula asked.

"You may not have heard me when I asked you if you had a basketball," Stone replied.

"No, I didn't!" Kerkula exclaimed. "Anyway, let's just wait around and see if someone will show up with a ball and we can begin our practice," Kerkula lamented.

"You guys can use this ball and play as long as 'that one' is not going to play," Fatu whispered softly as she tossed the Wilson brand basketball toward the court.

Heads turned as the voice softly echoed and hovered from behind the group of boys standing alongside the court. She was beautifully dressed and wearing a hot pink short pant and a white blouse that had the caption on the front, "Not this time, Maybe another day." She had on a pair of mixed-color pink and white tennis shoes that looked like a Michael Jordan brand with her hair folded up in a ponytail. She also wore light brown sunglasses that prevented others from seeing her eyes clearly. Around her neck was a high-priced African gold chain with her full name engraved on the locket. On her left hand was a ring that looked suspicious as though she has been engaged. There was no news concerning Fatu's engagement. At least, the rumor had not spread yet. She pulled the crowd by her presence as everyone seemed to have looked in the direction where she was standing.

Interestingly, Fatu once had a crush on Kerkula, but he did not find her attractive or someone he could date. She was practically young when she initially expressed her desire and likeness to be his friend. She always strived to come in his presence and be noticed. She often made complimentary gestures toward him, but he paid her no mind every time she tried. Fatu was under the impression that Kerkula liked her. She had been misinformed and misled by one of her best friends who told her in private, he was madly interested in her. This was a calculated lie by her friend to embarrass her publicly. Apparently, the friend was jealous and wanted to make sure that Kerkula directed his attention to her instead of Fatu. Coincidentally, both girls were infatuated with Kerkula at the same time, unbeknownst to each other. However, he remained absentminded to their individual intentions.

The friend who misled her always felt jealous about Fatu. She believed Fatu was born with a silver spoon in her mouth. In order words, Fatu's parents spoiled her by giving her all that she ever asked of them. She always believed Fatu was beautiful and boys liked her more than any other girl in town. Fatu never learned about the lie her friend had told her. She lived with the deception and took it personally against Kerkula throughout her interactions with him. In fact, she thought Kerkula felt he was "big and bad" and no girl could get to him. So, she decided to date Frankie instead to make Kerkula envious and subsequently go after her.

A couple of minutes after the practice started without Kerkula on the court, Frankie arrived and was immediately asked to join one of the teams already playing. This infuriated a good friend of Kerkula who was a bystander and not practicing. He demanded that Kerkula be allowed to practice even though Fatu had said no because the basketball belonged to her. Soon, there was talk going back and forth between Kerkula's friend and Fatu's. Suddenly, Frankie jumped in and wanted to fight Kerkula's friend who instigated the conflict. Kerkula had no other choice but to protect and advocate on his friend's behalf. This infuriated Fatu and she demanded her basketball back.

A fight quickly erupted among the boys and everyone got involved. Frankie accused Kerkula of inciting the fight and disrespecting his girlfriend. Frankie believed Kerkula was jealous of him for dating Fatu and wanted to put up a fight in her presence so that she would become discouraged and break up with him. A priest from the Catholic Diocese who had come to watch the practice quickly intervened and brought the boys to a short "come to Jesus talk." He was instrumental in resolving their differences and encouraged them to be friends and not enemies. He told the boys that the Bible as recorded in James 4:5 teaches men to love one another and not become enemies.

Memories of all the twists and turns in his friendship with Frankie began pulling through his mind as he sat in the car reminiscing about all that had transpired and what was about to happen to his dear friend. He couldn't withstand the tears falling from his eyes as Frankie disappeared slowly among the crowd that had gathered at the Brooklyn Police Station. He felt sad and guilty for leaving a friend behind, knowing that he was making a mistake to stay in Gbarnga and face the giant, the war. Let's go, Kerkula politely told the driver as he slowly made the turn onto the paved road headed toward Monrovia.

They drove all morning toward Kakata going through several towns and local communities along the way. Some towns and communities had checkpoints and others didn't. Some of the checkpoints were newly erected while others like the Iron Gate in Gbarnga and checkpoint in Salala had been there originally before the rebels' invasion. Even though there was evidence of pandemonium in some of the towns, none was a direct result of rebel activities emanating from Nimba County. Instead, the noise was pretty much a result of local merchants and market-goers who were transacting business as usual in the marketplace.

Typically, the marketplaces in Liberia are loud. One may almost think just by getting closer or entering a regular market and seeing the interactions among sellers and buyers that a crisis has unfolded or what we usually say, "all hell has broken loose." Notwithstanding, the market women understood this dynamic about their daily transactions with each other so much so that having major conflicts among themselves was almost unheard of or anticipated. Though there are times when hustling and bustling may have occured resulting in small skirmishes, the traditional and cultural will of the market women to do business and provide for their individual families often took preeminence over egoism and individualism.

Unlike previous checkpoints along the way, there were more military and paramilitary personnel at the checkpoint in Salala than he had seen anywhere else. There were police officers, Immigration & Customs officials, AFL soldiers, and other plainclothes individuals who referred to themselves as "detectives." They were beautifully attired and seemed little more professional and socially interactive with the civilian population. They took the time to give information to those who were fleeing the violence and headed toward Monrovia. They even took time to caution those who were headed toward the primary locations of the incursion. On the contrary to this prominent level of professionalism exhibited by the security personnel at the Salala checkpoint, it became evident that one of the newly erected checkpoints right outside the town of Gbatala proved that there was no need for another checkpoint in this area.

The checkpoint in Gbatala was a little different and awkward as compared to any of the other checkpoints along the way that they had already passed. This was mainly because the attitudes of the security guards at this checkpoint provoked Kerkula's annoyance. He became curious to know the reason why there was a checkpoint at this site. He had assumed to know the answer to his curiosity but wanted to verify if there were other hidden reasons for the additional checkpoints that had been erected along the Gbarnga-Monrovia Highway. He believed finding an answer to his curiosity wouldn't only confirm his assumption of what he already knew but would have cleared his doubts. It would have also prepared him mentally for the challenges ahead of them. He was convinced that these checkpoints never existed, even though time had elapsed since he traveled to Monrovia on those same roads.

He jumped right out of the moving 504 as the driver pulled slowly along the right side of the road, closer to the checkpoint. He walked straight toward the guards sitting in a small zinc hut, which they had erected at the gate. The hut was used as an office and as a protection from the blazing sun. It was also used to hide their identities from oncoming motorists and potential enemies.

"Excuse me, sir! Is there a problem here?" Kerkula asked.

"No sir! There is no problem. But you need to pass through an inspection before your car is allowed to go through the gate!" one of the security guards replied.

"I just went through inspection at the Salala gate, so why do I need another inspection?" Kerkula responded.

"Well, sir, let me tell you something, your 'Pekin them' have to eat, so give us 'something' so we can open the gate for you," another guard quickly responded.

"This is too much and unnecessary. I am not giving you any more money!" Kerkula insisted in a loud and trembling voice.

The driver sensed that his customer, Kerkula, was becoming agitated and very soon his anger would have led to a confrontation with the guards.

He quickly hopped out of the 504 and ran to the gate where Kerkula was involved in an intense conversation with the guards, going back and forth.

"Just give them something small—a bribe! So, we can get out of here. It is getting late and we still have a long way to go," the driver pleaded with Kerkula. "Besides, things are becoming worse over here and I have to return home tonight," the driver whispered in Kerkula's ear.

"Why do I have to keep spending my money at these gates?" Kerkula asked rhetorically. "I just spent almost one hundred Liberian dollars (LD) at the gate in Gbarnga and another two hundred dollars (LD) at Salala. Why should I spend any more money here?" Kerkula lamented. "In fact, this gate is totally unnecessary. Giving them money is like giving it to waste," Kerkula insisted further.

"But we need to go! As I said earlier, it is getting late. I need to go quickly and return to Gbarnga before night falls," the driver appealed to Kerkula.

"Ok, if you insist that I give them money! I will, but it would be a percentage of your rental agreement," Kerkula replied.

"Ok, fine!" the driver responded, harshly.

He was becoming frustrated with the entire back-and-forth between Kerkula and the fighters. They had insisted on receiving a bribe from him before opening the gate to allow their car to go through, but Kerkula was not willing to spend any additional money at the gate or any other gates for that matter. What he failed to realize was there were still more gates ahead of them and spending more time at one gate arguing or refusing to give a bride was not a smart move to take. It would further delay their estimated time of arrival in Harbel and not allow enough time for the driver to return home to his family, especially during the daylight. There is an adage in Liberia which says, "The night has many visitors that no one knows or can easily see from whence they come. So, driving late at night especially alone may eventually lead you into their paths and there are no guaranteed outcomes of your encounter with them."

Unfortunately, bribery is not a strange phenomenon in Liberia. Interestingly, it is becoming or has already become a widespread cultural norm or a way of life among Liberians. It is beginning to spread rapidly like wildfire from individual to individual, institution to institution and most sadly, the church is no exception. It is not that the vicious cycle of bribery had not existed in Liberia before. It has been for decades but was practiced at some level of civility, reverence for the constitution, and decency in society. The spike in bribery has been mostly influenced by illegal foreign nationals, especially those from the African Sub-Regions who have come into the country to conduct trade and commerce and are conducting it illegally. The influx of foreigners has not only encouraged and made bribery an acceptable way of life among Liberians, it has promoted an increased level of corruption in every sector of the country including the church.

This is not to be pessimistic or decry anyone in any farcical ways. Some Liberians, especially those with certain authority and leadership power are comfortable extracting money from the less fortunate in society or forcing them to give brides for their own rights and privileges. Sometimes, they even go further, denying others their rightful opportunities as Liberians. No one, not even the foreigners who reside in Liberia, is exonerated from this "hand of evil," as I would like to call it, which has and continues to force others against their will by extracting bribes from them. We have become even more comfortable forcing others or making them to give us their hard-earned money for their rights and privileges they deserve in the first place.

The perpetual masterminding of corrupt practices by Liberians and our foreign brothers and sisters who reside within our territorial borders or do business with the country from afar can only be abolished when Liberians stand up against it. The abolition of corruption must first start with us as Liberians for others to see and know that we are serious about making a change. It is a shame on some of those in authority for encouraging the wide spread of bribery. It has become a systemic epidemic and is actively infesting both our public and private sectors. This infestation is eroding the values that had separated and distinguished Liberia from the community of nations in Africa. In some cases, the elderly in society are the most vulnerable when it comes to some of these egoistic bribe-extracting behaviors. Elderly individuals are easy targets for those who are often found abusing their authority. Because the elderly usually don't like to argue and do not have time to complain, they are easily targeted and exploited.

Hesitantly, Kerkula reached down into his back pocket and pulled out a five-dollar (U.S.) bill and gave it to the commander, hoping to get some cash back but he didn't. The commander insisted there was no money on site to give Kerkula his balance. Moreover, he said, "We do not give change to anyone when they hand us money. This is not a marketplace or money-changing booth. We are soldiers at war and not businessmen," the Commander added. He turned around and began to walk back to his office. Suddenly, Kerkula noticed that the gate was wide opened after he had handed the money to the Commander. He became even more agitated when the Commander walked away leaving him standing without his cash balance. Unfortunately, there was absolutely nothing he could do to get his balance but to walk away angry. In a twinkle of an eye, the Commander and his security guards had an instant change of attitude toward Kerkula and his driver after receiving the bribe as though the initial interactions between them had not occurred.

Both men drove through the opened gate and never cared to look back. The driver stepped harder on the accelerator in frustration as the 504 spun quickly on the gravel road leaving dust and dried debris flying in the air. Swiftly but surely, the 504 disappeared out of sight. The Commander and his guards wondered what had happened to Kerkula and his driver. "He must have been driving presumably 90 miles per hour on 65-mile-per-hour roads," the Commander thought to himself as he held his head in his hand. "Maybe the driver is angry with us for delaying his customer or taking his money," one of the guards said scornfully. "We don't care, if it makes him upset, let him come here and say something to me."

"We will see who has the power!" another guard added in a braggadocios manner.

45 Minutes to Kakata

His driver must have been still angry from the interactions at the checkpoint in Gbatala as they began the drive to Kakata, the point of intersection where they had to exit and began the final leg of their journey to Harbel. It took them only forty-five minutes, nonstop from Salala checkpoint to the dusty city of Kakata. He drove as fast as he could, approximately 90 miles an hour, as though he was driving a Shanghai maglev or the Harmony CRH 380A.

The drive to Kakata was quiet and peaceful. There were not many movements of people along the roads or even the nearby towns. There was relative peace and calm throughout the drive as though nothing was happening on the other side of the country. Neither Kerkula nor his driver had to stop at a checkpoint or give anyone money whatsoever. Kerkula spent most of his time listening to music on the national radio while his driver drove. Apparently, listening to music through the drive helped both men cope with their stress from the earlier encounter with the guards in Gbatala.

HARBEL, FIRESTONE

In one of the towns along the way, there were young boys playing soccer while on the other side of the road just beneath the town where the boys were playing was a group of females, both old and young at the creekside. Some were braiding hair and fetching water while others were washing clothes and dirty dishes. Traditionally, in Liberia, the local creeksides are used for several reasons. Typically, villagers, especially the young girls and boys will go down to the creek during the morning and evening hours to fetch water. The water from the running streams or creeks is usually carried back to town mostly in zinc buckets or enamel dishes that are purchased from the local marketplace. Often, their parents, mostly the mothers, would use the water brought from the creeks and streams for four major reasons.

First, the water is used to complete early morning and late evening baths for the adults, mainly the father who is the primary breadwinner of the family and the mother who is the main caretaker and peacemaker by virtue of implied cultural and traditional perceptions. Notice this statement, the fetched water would be used to take baths and not showers because taking showers are not common in the interiors or rural areas of Liberia. In fact, taking baths at home or the creekside is considered a cultural way of life and is practiced mostly by those found in the rural areas and even some urban dwellers who cannot afford the purchase and use of showers. After the parents have taken their baths, the kids would have to use whatever water that is left to take their baths. Often, the kids would most likely take their baths at the creeks or streams first before bringing water to town to avoid the hustle and bustle of everyone taking a bath at home. Nevertheless, if the temperature falls and it becomes increasingly cold, the kids would have to make additional trips to the creeks to meet the demand for bath water for all household members.

Second, the water that the kids bring home is also used for drinking. Prior to now, and even now, most rural homes in Liberia do not have electricity for domestic or public use. Few of the homes that might have electricity in rural areas are probably the properties of senior government officials, high-earned-income families or businessmen. Typical rural households can hardly afford to sustain their families by meeting basic daily necessities like food, shelter, and clothing. How much more can they afford the costs of operating a private generator to supply electricity for the use of household appliances?

Traditionally, water brought from the creeks is treated by pouring it in aluminum made pots or handmade clay pots to heat up in order to reduce

25

the likelihood of germs and cold water bacterial agents like vibrio cholera, serovarieties O1 and O139 that have the potential of causing cholera, Vibrio parahaemolyticus, which causes gastroenteritis; Salmonella enterica subsp, Enterica serovar paratyphi, Salmonella enteric subsp, Enterica serovar typhi, and Salmonella enterica subsp, Enterica serovar typhimurium, which have the potential of causing typhoid fever, and other serious salmonellosis; Shigella dysenteries, Shigella flexneri, Shigella boydii, Shigella sonnei, which have the potential of causing bacillary dysentery or shigellosis, and Escherichia coli, particularly serotypes such as O148, O157, and O124, which have the potential of causing acute diarrheas and gastroenteritis. Some interior dwellers are not aware of the existence of these water bacteria. They do not consider the heating of water as any form of treatment against the bacteria that exist. Instead, they see it as a normal way of life.

According to the World Health Organization (WHO) 2018 factsheets on drinking water, 844 million people lack even a basic drinking-water service, including 159 million people who are dependent on surface water. The WHO indicated that the transmission of water-borne diseases such as cholera, diarrhea, dysentery, hepatitis A, typhoid, and polio are a result of contaminated water and poor sanitation. The WHO also estimates that approximately 842,000 people die each year from diarrhea due to unsafe drinking water, sanitation, and hand hygiene (WHO, 2018).

Liberia is among some developing countries in Africa that are currently struggling with poor health conditions due to the lack of adequate healthcare programs and a deteriorating healthcare system. The governments of some of these African countries including Liberia do not allocate enough funding in their fiscal budget on healthcare. Some do not see healthcare for its citizens as a national priority or the lack of healthcare as a national health crisis. Some African governments have a misconception that investment in health does not necessarily contribute to the growth and development of the country or economy. Some African governments believe spending on other sectors like security, infrastructure, road networks is much more essential than health. Though they may talk about the need to invest in healthcare or develop a standardized healthcare system, much of the discussions are politically driven and reduced to theoretical applications (writings) and not necessarily implementations.

According to a United Nation Economic Commission for Africa (UNECA) 2018 Report, Africa has 15 percent of the global population but carries one-fourth of the global disease burden. Nearly 60 percent of

Africa's population lives in slums while the continent spends only 6.5 to 7.8 billion dollars, which equals to approximately 15 percent of government budget on health.

In September 2000, at the Abuja Declaration, there were 189 African heads of state who made promises of commitment and solidarity to improve social and economic conditions in the world's poorest nations by 2015. Among the eight goals set at the declaration, three were health related, with an additional two goals having some health component. Unfortunately, to date, only five African countries, including Zambia, Rwanda, Madagascar, Togo, and Botswana, have met their respective commitments to the Abuja Declaration. This is a clear manifestation that the misconception among African leaders not to invest in health is being considered seriously.

Some African governments would go on airways, write in newspapers, or even make major annual addresses on the issue of healthcare for its citizens to appeal to the outside world or portray a good image of their leadership as a way of soliciting foreign financial assistance. Once the funds are allocated and disbursed to these governments, accountability becomes a nightmare and eventually history. The sad truth is, a good percentage of these governments have no healthcare initiatives meant to benefit ordinary citizens. Some Liberians believe that government failure to initiate a standardized health delivery system is rooted in the concept that typical Liberians would prefer traditional health practices over modern medicine. Whatever the case may be, there must be a balance between modern medicine and traditional health practices for citizens who prefer one practice to the other. In such a technological era, the practices or acceptance of traditional medicine above modern medicine almost doesn't exist and might be considered an unrealistic approach.

According to a United Nations International Children's Emergency Fund (UNICEF) 2009 report, one in eight children dies before reaching the age of five, children remain highly vulnerable to diarrhea. A 2007 Demographic and Health Survey showed that only two-thirds of Liberians have access to safe drinking water. In both rural and urban areas, there is a risk that water may be contaminated because of fourteen years of civil war which destroyed much of the country's infrastructure. In 2008, another study conducted by the government of Liberia and UNICEF indicated that only 8 percent of Liberia's 4.7 million population had access to piped running water which was primarily gathered from sources like water wells and

A JOURNEY TO BONG MINES

not the National Water & Sewer Plant that is responsible to supply pipe-borne drinking water to local communities.

The third use of creek or stream water that is brought home by children is to cook. Because most homes in rural areas do not have piped, boiled water systems, creek water is used in its natural state without any purifications or water treatments when cooking household meals. "Domestic or Household Managers," as I would like to call our mothers, would literally use the creek water to prepare their foods and cook with it without any hesitations. Some mothers are aware of the dangers of cooking with creek water that has not been treated or chemically processed before use while others are not. They don't have a choice but to use creek water and survive. This has been an acceptable practice for decades and is being practiced even to this date. Some of the homes that are educated on these issues or are fortunate to have some modern water treatments or disinfectant products, for example water treatment substances approved by the United States Environmental Protection Agency (EPA) or the World Health Organization (WHO), like chlorine, chlorine dioxide, ozone, monochloramine, or UV, would be cautious to first apply them to their water before using it. Unfortunately, due to the high illiteracy rate compounded with the excessive costs of living in Liberia, not everyone can afford to purchase and treat water supplies with a water-treatment chemical before use.

The fourth use of creek or stream water by rural homes is to complete household or family laundry. Because rural homes are not equipped with electricity that would allow the use of laundry washers and dryers, parents have mostly two choices to complete weekly or monthly household laundry; use fetched water at home or take the laundry to the creek or stream to complete them there. Fetching water to complete an entire household laundry at home depending on the size of a family and the distance from home to the creek or stream can be a daunting task for kids. It is one of the hardest chores for kids growing up. Kids are literally required to carry "water holding vessels" on their head back and forth for hours to make sure that all laundries are fully completed. Such home chores can make kids quickly irritated and disengaged with their parents especially if the task becomes an expected routine.

Ironically, there are Liberians who hold on to this misconception that one reason why some Liberians are "short in statue" or are "baldheaded" is attributed to the intensity of carrying water vessels on their bare head when they were growing up. On the contrary, completing laundry for an

28

entire household can be a fun chore for kids provided they can take the laundry to the creek or stream to complete them. Kids in rural areas like to play in running water while ignoring the dangers (e.g., germs, diseases, snakes) and other predators that are commonly found in and around running or still waters. Washing laundry could also be a fun chore for kids to complete if the home has a "water-well" where the kids could fetch water. Water-wells are common in rural areas and even some developing neighborhoods in urban areas.

They arrived in Kakata from Salala exactly forty-five minutes and decided to refuel the 504. They also decided to have lunch before heading to Harbel, their destination. Like Salala, Kakata was relatively calm but busy with market-goers as usual. The intersection at Bong Mines Road and Main Street was jam-packed with travelers, "money changers," "shoe-shine boys," retailers who are often called "waiter-market seller," and other vagrants or "down-and-out" individuals who walked the streets of Kakata daily. Traffic was always busy at this intersection, especially during weekdays and on Saturdays. There were several unauthorized packing stations along the roads intended to pick up passengers who were headed to different cities around the country. The unstructured and unauthorized arrangement of traffic activities within and around this area is one of the primary reasons for traffic congestion and continual movement of people.

Harbel, Here We Come!

Lunch seemed to have gone well and both men finally appeared lively and excited as they boarded their vehicle for the last leg of their trip. The driver seemed to have lost track of time and the fact that it was getting late. He had to return the same day to his family in Gbarnga. He reminded Kerkula about his return to Gbarnga several times from whence they began the trip. Now, it appeared as though being in a calm and peaceful city made the difference from how he felt initially. He pushed the key into the ignition and turned the car on. A smile ran across his face as he looked sideways toward Kerkula.

"What is it?" Kerkula asked.

"Are you doing ok?" the driver asked.

"Who? Me? Yes! I am!" Kerkula replied confidently. "I just have too much on my mind, right now. That's all!" Kerkula continued.

A JOURNEY TO BONG MINES

"I know! It will be alright. It will soon be over, and we'll be there," the driver whispered.

"I am not really concerned about the driving. I am really concerned about all that is happening right now in our country," Kerkula murmured. "I am not sure what is going to happen in the next couple of months. I am not even sure what is going to happen to our families, loved ones, and friends," Kerkula continued. "What about Frankie and his parents, brothers, and sisters? I am not sure if he gets it yet!" Kerkula said softly as his voice began to tremble and his eyes turned blood red like the sight of the evening sunset.

"What do you mean by 'he doesn't get it yet?'" the driver asked.

"Frankie seems not to understand rebel activities or what a military coup is all about. I think he is confused about the difference between the two and has considered the rebel incursion as though it was a military coup, which could occur within a brief time frame," Kerkula added. "He might be totally confused. I am worried that he and his family might lose their lives thinking they can withstand the whirlwind of the rebels' incursion," Kerkula answered. "There are also other friends and neighbors that are making no plans to seek safety elsewhere, hoping that the war will not reach them or may pass them by without any problems. Maybe, they have nowhere to go, who knows!" Kerkula added.

"There is not much we can do but to pray for them and even ourselves. There are no guarantees that we've landed on safe shores," the driver said tearfully.

They went back and forth reminiscing about their pasts and emotionally discussing what was yet to come. They thought about how bad it would be for innocent families and individuals who had nowhere to go. They also talked passionately about their individual families as though they had known each other for many years. I guess they became comfortable with each other after driving for a while and encountering some setbacks along the way. All seemed to have been going well further into the drive to Harbel. As they drove through local towns and rubber farms, they came across villagers and workers from the Firestone Rubber Plantation Company going about their normal lives as though the news about the rebels' advancements toward the plantation had not reached them or been broadcast on the national radio. One would easily forget that they had just driven from a troubled environment just by driving through the towns, villages, and rubber trees and seeing how normal people were going about their lives.

HARBEL, FIRESTONE

As they drove along the roads, they came to a place called "Dolo's Town" just fifteen minutes walking distance outside the city limits of Harbel. Dolo's town is not too far from another local town called "Bawehn." Both towns are practically located in proximity which allows their residents to go back and forth between towns. There were also other small towns like Peter's Town, Unification Village, Beon, Peabody Farm, Batro, and others around Harbel.

Further along the drive, they came across several young boys standing alongside the road with sugar canes in their hands for sale. Kerkula and his driver pull up along the road because they wanted to purchase some. The boys had some of the brightest yellow and juicy-looking sugar canes that he had ever seen. Seeing the sugar canes, Kerkula couldn't resist his desire to quench his thirst by biting into one. He reached down in his pockets and pulled out two five-dollar liberty bills (local Liberian currency) and handed them to one of the boys. He purchased two of the sugar canes and gave one to his driver. Both men cleaned and cut the sugar canes into pieces at the site of the purchased, sat in the car and ate almost all of it before driving home.

Once upon a time, Kerkula had expressed his love for sugarcane. He often told a tale that his father once shared with him about the importance of sugar cane and how it can be an essential supplement for food especially when food is not available or in short supply. His father once told him that he had to depend on raw sugarcane juice for twenty-one days. He vividly remembered his father telling him how they were airlifted and dropped somewhere in the forest of Grand Gedeh County during month-long combat trainings. The trainings were being conducted as Liberia prepared to receive heads of state from forty-eight African nations along with three thousand delegates who were gathering for the 16th Annual Summit of the Organization of African Unity (OAU) at the OAU Village outside the Liberian capital of Monrovia.

Everyone was home as their 504 slowly came to a stop in front of the house he called home. For more than five years, his father had been assigned as the commander of the military unit deployed in Harbel. His father commanded a small group of military personnel that worked together with PPD to provide security and protection to the entire Firestone Plantation.

He carried one of many bags from the 504 as he made his way up the stairs toward the front door. He pulled the screen door and knocked twice but no one answered or opened the door. He heard voices of people that sounded familiar to him and thought there must have been a party going on in the house. He quickly remembered that his father was not a huge fan of a house party. So, he changed his mind and proceeded to knock on the door for the second time. The curtain to the living room window pulled aside and a familiar face appeared in front of the glass. It was his little half-sister. She shouted his name ecstatically, "Oldman! Oldman! Oh, Oldman [as he was affectionately called] has come"; her voice penetrated the house. It immediately caused everyone to become concerned as though something terrible had happened. She struggled to catch her breath and balance but managed to reach the door and opened it for her brother before anyone could make their way to the front door.

Everyone seemed happy to see him. They gave him hugs, kisses, and began to dance. They acted in their usual frenzy of jumping around and talking. The family normally engages in this tradition when one of its members who had been gone away for sometimes comes back. As the celebration quieted, he became more and more concerned that his father was nowhere to be found. He was not in the room with everyone else. He hurried to his bedroom but did not see him. He also went to the back yard and looked under the almond tree, his father's favorite sitting place especially during the dry season but did not see him either. He quickly turned around and went back up the stairs and asked his stepmother, "Where is the 'papay' [dad]?"

"You know your father. He is probably somewhere around helping someone as usual," his stepmother replied. "He left for work this morning and has not returned. I think he is still at the office helping some of his soldiers," his stepmother continued. "Maybe, he might be on his way back home now," she added.

"Oh, okay! I will wait for him to come home instead of going to find him at the office," Kerkula responded.

"That's an innovative idea, Oldman!" she concluded.

It was common in their family to call each other by nicknames rather than their legal names, especially during family gatherings. This was one way of demonstrating family ties and values which helped to simplify their relationship with each other and kept the fuel of the family burning. For example, they called their father "Papay," Kerkula "Oldman," and their oldest brother "J-man." They also called their stepmother "Oldma" instead of her rank in the family.

As he turned around to walk away from the conversation with his stepmother, someone slipped a key in the lock on the front door. As the front door began to open an image appeared in the doorway. It was their father. He had no clue that his son had arrived in Harbel. He moved quickly and gave his father a hug before taking his briefcase from him and took it into the living room. His father chatted with him for a couple of minutes before he slipped into the bathroom for his evening shower. Their father seemed tired and sleepy after eating dinner. Therefore, he decided to go to bed. Kerkula hung around the living room for a while watching television with his little brothers and cousins before going to bed at midnight.

The night was peaceful and relatively quiet. Harbel was noted for its lively atmosphere where young boys and girls walked the streets usually in the moonlight. Moviegoers drove back and forth from the movie theaters with no fear. Some residents even visited Monrovia during weekends to hang out and came home late at night without fear. But this began to change as the next few nights seemed different than usual. The community became too quiet as though the city had been engulfed or captured by evil spirits. His father woke up early the next morning to get ready for his daily workday routine. He had to be at his office to meet with two groups of people to settle an alleged domestic abuse involving a visiting soldier and a local taxi driver. He had to give Kerkula specific instructions on the trip he and his brother had to make to "Waterside," a densely populated marketplace in the heart of Monrovia. So, he went to his room and woke him up. He gave him some money and told him exactly what he needed to be done. He boarded his military jeep and drove out to work.

A Trip to Waterside—Monrovia

Kerkula had come to Harbel from Gbarnga at the request of his father for two reasons. He was asked to bring some of the important household materials that were left in Gbarnga for safe keeping in Harbel. His father had hoped that the incursion wouldn't have reached Firestone and the things brought over would have been secured. The second and most important reason for Kerkula's visit to Harbel was to take one of his younger brothers, the one who was next to him in their family rankings, to shop for footwear in downtown Waterside.

Early that morning after their father had left for work, Kerkula and his brother bade the other members of the family goodbye and boarded a taxi to Monrovia. As usual, Waterside was jam-packed to capacity, more than the area could spaciously accommodate. People were literally rubbing against one another as they walked past each other. Kerkula had visited Waterside several times on separate occasions prior to this trip. He had a memory of the hustle and bustle one had to go through in trying to get in and out of the area especially when constrained with time. In fact, he was born and raised in PHP, Monrovia, next to Salt Beach. He grew up going down to Waterside to shop and sometimes walk the streets with his friends or siblings. He was very much aware of the environment and could easily tell you where to find goods and services without any difficulty. Some of his friends called him, "Cookies" because of his appealing abilities and ever-smiling face. He had a way of engaging people very well and maintained a photographic memory of street signs and landmarks.

After several hours of being in downtown Waterside, they returned home with a pair of new shoes for his brother. They had gone to Waterside only to purchase a pair of shoes and nothing else. His brother had expressed his desire for a new pair of shoes that he could use for church and other outgoing activities. So, their father wanted to make sure that he purchased a pair of shoes for him as a token of appreciation for his helpfulness and care for his siblings.

Their father arrived home later that evening and was pleased with how Kerkula conducted the trip to Monrovia and the shoes they'd purchased. As usual, he sat in the living room and chatted with his boys for a while before leaving to take his evening shower. He went straight to bed upon his return from the shower because he was tired as he was the day before. Kerkula, his brothers, and cousins decided to spend the rest of the evening quietly together. They went in the front yard and sat on the stairs to enjoy the moonlight and watch groups of passersby. After sitting outside for a while, they decided to go to bed as the night became cooler and darker. One-by-one, the nightwalkers disappeared into their homes and the streets became empty. The city had finally returned to its peaceful and quiet nature. By midnight, the streets became completely cleared and darkness filled the sky. The shadows of streetlights began to fade away as the early morning dew fell. There were not many cars in the streets. As usual, after midnight, the most common cars found in the streets belong to the PPD. They would usually stay up patrolling the streets till the break of day. Their presence in the streets provided lasting assurance to residents of Harbel and nearby villages.

Early the next morning as the sun began to rise from the northern end of the city, the dew quickly dissipated and business, as usual, was back in full swing. School kids, market-goers, rubber farmers, PPD personnel, and even sanitation workers were back on their usual routine. For some odd reasons, the city seemed overpopulated suddenly. To his knowledge, there were too many people in town that he had physically seen. There were people walking and standing all along the roads especially on the field at the open theater area where the community came out to watch free movies every Friday on the big screen. Normally, Harbel was populated on paydays and other special days that were celebrated like Christmas, Independence Day, or New Year's Day. But on this day, June 5, 1990, he could not figure out why there were so many people in town. Some of the people walking the streets were familiar; some lived in the community and were frequent in the day-to-day activities. There were some who came from the housing communities on nearby divisions where rubber farmers lived and worked. He could easily differentiate strangers from residents who walked the streets daily because of the clothes they wore, their interactions with each other, and manner in which they conducted themselves.

It was almost easy to tell a Firestone worker from strangers or ordinary people who had just come through Harbel or moved to town newly. He liked to call them "Firestone workers" or employees of Firestone instead of using the derogative term "rubber tappers," which they were often called. Some of the so-called visitors or those who felt they had better jobs or enjoyed better living conditions compared to the farmers would often call them by such derogative name as a way of becoming spiteful or humiliating. Evidently, Firestone did not do an excellent job in providing better housing for the average worker on the plantation.

The average workers were literally forced to live in tight-spaced one- or two-bedroom apartments provided by the company. They also had to endure the repugnant smell of daily harvested rubber. They were given no other options of accommodations. The only other options of leaving those living apartments were either to resign or work your way up through the rank and file of management which would have automatically changed the dynamics of one's employment status. Realistically, this was almost unachievable or unrealizable for the average workers. However, it was a dream come true for the fortunate few who may have gained some level of favor with their bosses or established some interconnectedness within the system. Interestingly, Firestone workers had a unique pride about who they were and the job they did. Their proud mannerisms and work ethics did not stem from upbeat arrogance but pleasant dispositions. It was also based on the mere fact that they had a job that allowed them to generate income and provide for their individual families.

They were undeniably proud to be Liberians who, regardless of the kind of work they did for a living, were able to contribute individually and collectively to the socioeconomic development of the country. Another way one could identify a Firestone worker was by the yellow raincoats, boots, and safety gears they wore during and sometimes off work hours. This is not meant to decry the kind of job the workers did. Evidently, there were times when one could not easily separate the worker from the work or invite the worker without considering the distinctive smell of the work he did. Literally, one couldn't easily divorce the two. They were almost uniquely intertwined.

Unusual Sounds! Strange People!

The number of people in the streets continued to increase profoundly by the minute. No one seemed to have noticed or at least sensed any signs of danger of what was unfolding gradually around them. Surprisingly, an old friend to one of his father's adopted sons suddenly showed up on the stair in front of their house. This old friend once upon a time spent lots of time with them in Sanniquelle, Nimba County, where his father was once assigned. His name was Tony. He was a good friend to Kerkula's adopted brother, Saye.

Several years ago in the early 1980s, just few months after President William R. Tolbert Jr. was assassinated by seventeen enlisted men of the Armed Forces of Liberia (AFL) under the newly adopted name, The People's Redemption Council (PRC). His father was transferred from the Barclay's Training Center (BTC) in Monrovia to Nimba County in the northern region of Liberia. It was in Sanniquelle that his father met and adopted Saye as his son. Saye visited their home frequently and made himself at home. It was during one of Saye's frequent visits to Kerkula's parents' home that he introduced Tony as his best friend.

Tony quickly became no stranger to Kerkula's parents and the entire family. Just as Saye was privileged to visit as much as he wanted, so was Tony. He seemed to have been a decent man and carried himself modestly among his peers in the community. Tony also seemed to have been good at physically demanding work. In fact, he was incredibly helpful during the construction of Kerkula parent's home in Gbarnga in the late 1980s. Kerkula's parents trusted and respected him not only because he was the friend of their son but because he had a good moral compass and exemplified true character. Moral compass has been defined as the inner voice that tells us what we should and should not do in various circumstances (Bennett, 1995; Huntsman, 2010).

Tony's sudden appearance on the stairs at the front door left everyone a little surprised and concerned. He seemed a little bemused but became alert by the presence of the entire family together in one place. He was calmed and had a smile on his face as he climbed the stairs and greeted Kerkula first, the Oldma next, and everyone else. As he began to talk, his hands began to quiver, his body grew tense, and his eyes oscillated as he watched the movement of people from one place to another. He paid more attention to the movements of people especially in one of the neighborhoods that were predominantly inhibited by Northern and Southeastern Liberians.

He was quick to ask for Kerkula's father. He wanted to see and talk with him urgently. Unfortunately, the Oldman was not home yet from work. He looked in Kerkula's face and said to him, "You all need to find a place to go. It is no longer safe here, and we don't know what is about to happen anytime now or over the next few days. You will do yourselves a big favor if you began to pack your bags and leave this house. I cannot tell you what is about to happen or who is about to do what, but I know what is coming is not good and you don't want to waste any time getting out of here," Tony added.

His rendition of what was coming instantly mounted panic in almost everyone listening to him. Sadly, no one, not even Kerkula could easily bring himself to figure out what needed to be done momentarily. The urgency expressed in Tony's rendition forcefully superseded the need to be involved in anything else but take immediate actions. Unfortunately, their father was not home yet to give further directions.

Tony bade them goodbye and gave his final advice, "Take what is coming seriously and act now!" He turned his back and began to walk down the stairs. In a twinkle of an eye, he disappeared in the crowd and no one laid eyes on him again. As the family struggled to compose themselves and make sense of what they'd just heard from Tony, there was a squeak in the back door. It was their father who had just returned home from work. He greeted them and went directly to his bedroom. A couple of minutes later, he came out with a change of clothes. Initially, he was dressed up in his camouflage uniform but upon his return from his bedroom, he was wearing a pair of khaki pants, a white T-shirt and some flip-flops. He called for a drink of water and immediately began to reveal some information about the incursion.

He seemed relaxed and not troubled as he shared the information with his family. He informed them that the management of Firestone Rubber Plantation had assured the workers and security personnel that there would be no need to panic. He said, "Management informed us that they were in constant and direct contact with the leadership of the rebel movement who had assured them there would be no occupation of the facility." Accordingly, management had assured workers and security personnel that the rebels were headed directly to Monrovia and were not interested in branching out through Firestone.

His meeting with the family lasted a couple of minutes. Everyone except one person seemed pretty much convinced that management would do its best to protect the plantation by preventing the rebels from going through or occupying it. Kerkula was not convinced that it was possible for the rebels to head directly to Monrovia without branching out through Harbel or another part of the plantation. He had no military training or insight. Like his father, he was very keen on listening to the BBC *Focus on Africa* news program and practically followed the activities of the rebels from the beginning of the incursion to the advancements made from city to city. Kerkula knew that the rebels' seizure of Firestone Rubber Plantation was evidently part of their strategic plan. Their leader, Mr. Taylor, had alluded to the plan in some form or fashion during his radio interviews with BBC *Focus on Africa* broadcaster Robin White after the city of Kakata fell to rebel control and the pursuit of Monrovia was initiated.

It didn't make any sense whatsoever that the rebels would have advanced to Monrovia directly without capturing Firestone and maintaining it as one of its operational bases. Unlike other cities already captured, they needed Firestone for several reasons. Not only was Firestone closer and connected to Monrovia geographically by paved roads, it also provided essential logistics including vehicles, fuel and gasoline, and other equipment that the rebels needed the most to transport their men and supplies of arms and ammunition to the men in the front lines. It also had an abundance of food, medical supplies, and hospital (e.g., Duside Hospital) equipped to provide the necessary food supplies and needed medical care for wounded soldiers and civilians alike.

Another reason why it was impossible for the rebels to have gone directly to Monrovia without capturing and maintain Firestone was the fact that the company had some level of standardized communication capabilities. The availability of such a system of communication allowed the rebel leadership to conduct radio propaganda and met other communication needs, especially with the local population and the outside world. This was one aspect of the propaganda strategy Mr. Taylor utilized to his advantage and psychologically captured the minds of Liberians at home and abroad. He mounted the airways weekly on BBC *Focus on Africa* with Robin White discussing their plans, advances, and successful operations.

Firestone seemed to have been in the position to formulate new contractual agreements with the leadership of the movement based upon the terms and agreements of their needs. It was speculated by some Liberians that Firestone had the ability to make available huge sums of American dollars if a secure agreement was reached or a forceful demand was made by the rebels. Mr. Taylor and the leadership of the movement were fully aware that capturing and maintaining Firestone as a key territory would benefit them in several ways: (1) It would put them in a solid position to ensure continual cash flow which would have undoubtedly supported their strive to capture Monrovia. (2) It would give them added advantage in overthrowing the democratically elected government, no matter the costs. (3) It would have allowed them easy access and drive time to the Robert International Airport, Liberia's only international airport. (4) Firestone would have also served as a safe haven for the thousands of Liberians who were already trapped in Monrovia and its environs, making it easy for the rebels to capture the city with fewer atrocities and civilian casualties.

Kerkula understood, for the most part, the strategies the rebels used to advance in some of the cities that were previously captured. His adopted brother, Tony, told them about it and what signs to watch out for. Also, he spent most of his growing up around his father who talked with him one-on-one about his life in the military and what it meant to be a commissioned officer. His father loved and trusted him. He always spent time with him, teaching him about military sciences and the act of war. Besides spending time with his father and listening to *Focus on Africa*, Kerkula also read articles and other literature on rebel activities and the rules of engagement of war that had occurred in other countries. For example, rebel groups like the Al-Shabbab, the Tuareg rebels of Mail; the Lord's Resistance Amy of Uganda; the National Liberation Forces of Burundi; the West Side

Boys of Sierra Leone, the Forces for Liberation (FLR) of Rwanda, Boko Haram of Nigeria, the Congolese Revolutionary Movement of the Democratic Republic of Congo, etc.

Some of these rebel groups have been in existence for a significant period while others have only existed for a while. Some operated within the territorial jurisdictions of their respective countries, terrorizing their fellow citizens, while others have been operating from abroad. Kerkula thought it expedient after the civil unrest in Liberia to read a little more about rebel warfare first to gather a better understanding about the rationale behind their formation and activities of rebel groups and second to help educate others who may have no understanding of why rebel groups exist and what impact they have on society.

It was some time after midday; the sun stood overhead and was shining as bright as a blazing fire. Kerkula along with his family began to socialize after the talk with their father. He became a little uneasy due to the temperature in the house. Hence, he decided to go back out the front door and sit on the stairs to enjoy the movement of people in and out of the open field. He peeped through the window curtain facing the streets and became instantly astonished by what he saw. In the back of his mind, he thought he saw some strange people and unusual things happening on the other side of the open field. Overcome by curiosity and a desire to verify the information Tony had shared with them previously about what was coming, he decided to go out of the house. He opened the front door quickly and went outside. Instead of sitting down on the stairs, he decided to lay his back against the rail and stood on the third flat of stairs to clearly see what was really going on.

Suddenly, gunfire erupted. Not sure what sound it was and where exactly it came from, he stepped down two flats of stairs and took a clearer look in the direction where the gunfire supposedly came from. To his astonishment, his eyes met bizarre images. On one side of the street, there were men in clean camouflage with rusted artillery cannons mounted in battered pickup trucks, thin barefooted teenagers lugged rocket-propelled grenade launchers across their chests and in their hands. There were children under the age of a youth who carried AK-47s while others had machetes in their hands. It was interesting to see how some of the guns were taller and heavier than the youth and teenagers who carried them.

On the other side of the streets across from the open field, some of the rebels were spotted wearing scruffy ripped jeans and torn T-shirts, colorful women's wigs, skeletons of dead people and animals around their necks and on the hoods of the pickup trucks they were driving. Some also had rain boots, mismatched tennis shoes, and shower slippers (flip-flops) on their feet with pieces of red cloth tied around their arms, legs, and foreheads while others were beautifully dressed in dress shoes, military boots, and different shades of police, military, immigration, and other uniforms. Prior to this incident, while Kerkula and his family were still talking with their father in the house, news surfaced in the neighborhood about the rebels' crossing over the Farmington River at Owens Grove into Firestone farm (Firestone, 2014).

The news about the rebels' entry into Firestone brought mixed emotions; some residents of Harbel were excited to see a "rebel" for the first time while others were uncertain and terrified about what was yet to come. Apparently, those who seemed to have been uncertain and terrified were those who may have constantly listened to BBC *Focus on Africa* or followed the developments and activities of the rebels from the inception of the incursion to their arrival on the plantation. They must have either experienced some of the atrocities caused by all the fighting groups or may have seen individuals who became victims. The evidence from the victims suggested that the magnitude of the atrocities committed and all that was unfolding needed not to be taken lightly.

He sat patiently on the stairs and watched the unpredictable and dramatic warfare unfold right in front of his eyes. One thing Kerkula noticed, there were no military or paramilitary resistance to the rebels who called themselves "freedom fighters." For the most part, they captured Harbel almost entirely unopposed with zero military resistance. It would be logical to think that there must have been a collective agreement between the high commands of the rebel movement and Firestone as previously indicated. This may have been the main reason why there was no military resistance on the plantation.

As he continued to watch the movement of the so-called freedom fighters, more and more sporadic gunfire began to occur between the residential units. The gunfire soon became loud and louder and spread quickly toward the open fields. Innocent lives were lost as civilians sprang in different directions for their lives. A complete state of anarchy began to unfold as the shooting began to spread rapidly out of control. There was gunfire on every side of town. Civilians who ran toward the market or residential areas were trapped by the presence of fighters who were advancing from those directions. The fighters appeared so quickly and unexpectedly that it took more residents by surprise. It was evident that many residents in Harbel were unprepared for the arrival of the freedom fighters. Fortunately for Kerkula and his family, they were somewhat prepared and had firsthand information from their brother, Tony, which helped them with overcoming the anxiety, fear, and stress of all that was going on. The situation would have been different for Kerkula and his family had their brother not informed them initially about what was coming their way. Even with the firsthand information they had, they still had to make sound decisions to leave town safely.

CHAPTER THREE

Miracles in the Sunshine

He was not sure that the freedom fighters, who were mostly referred to as rebels, were as naive and unskillful militarily as some may have thought about them.

He believed the fighters knew who their enemies were and why they targeted them specifically. Even though innocent people lost their lives during the civil crisis, there were many Liberians who had been targeted from the onset of the war. No doubt, the fighters went searching first for their targeted individuals who were on their so-called "blacklists" based on their reconnaissance and plans. Unfortunately, many times during the search process, innocent Liberians were caught up in the mist of the plan implementation or were in the wrong place at the wrong time.

Kerkula knew that his father might have been one of many names on the so-called blacklists because he was the military commander in Harbel. He concluded that Tony's unexpected visit at their parents' home was intentional and that he had come on reconnaissance for the rebels. Kerkula believed Tony knew if he had not traveled ahead of the fighting rebel battalion, the insurgents would have mercilessly and indiscriminately murdered his parents, brothers, and sisters as was done to other families who had careers in the AFL, paramilitary organizations, and other tribal groups.

Tony's visit to Harbel ahead of the rebels was a "miracle in the sunshine." God had manifested his saving grace to his children on a bright sun-shining day. Kerkula knew that Tony's willingness to risk his life to save his family was a miracle from God and nothing else. No act of humanity or Tony's unexpected visit to the house saved the lives of Kerkula's family. They were truly saved by the grace of God. Tony was like a guardian angel sent by God to protect his family. God used him at the right time and for the right purpose. The scripture reminds us that God will command his angels concerning us to

A JOURNEY TO BONG MINES

guide us in all our ways; they will lift us in their hands, so that our feet will not strike against a stone (Ps 91:11–12 NIV). Also, he will command his angels concerning us, to guide us carefully (Luke 4:10 NIV).

Kerkula was still standing on the stairs in front of his father's house watching all that was happening before his eyes. For some reason, he became stagnant and couldn't get himself to escape the terrifying event occurring outside. A "small still" voice kept whispering in his ears to go in and tell his parents, brothers, sisters, and especially their father to flee from their home immediately. He gathered the strength to finally go in the house when he could no longer keep his eyes on what he was seeing. As he struggled to compose himself, he slipped and fell against the front door but finally made his way back up and into the house.

"Papay! Papay!" It was how they usually called their father. "We have to get out of here!" he shouted in a loud voice. "They are coming toward our house, and I am sure they are coming directly to us," he continued.

He quickly gathered his brothers and had them remove all military-related items including uniforms, boots, caps, paperwork, IDs, ducktails, and guns. He took the 32 revolver and 45 pistols and buried them in the drum of uncooked parboiled rice. He carried the uzi and machine guns up into the attic and positioned them at the eve of the roof. He did this so when the rebels climbed the attic, they wouldn't easily see the guns since they were more cumbersome than the pistols. He also buried the ducktails and IDs bearing the name Sirleaf in the same drum of uncooked parboiled rice. He struggled to dispose of the suitcases that had newly made traditional dress suits (higher height suits) as Liberians often called them. His father had been sewing these outfits periodically with his hard-earned monthly paychecks for his retirement. A sizable number of the outfits had already been sewed for both parents and were put away in additional suitcases in the house before the rebels' arrival. He had planned to retire from the AFL and move back to Gbarnga the year after the rebels invaded Liberia.

Once upon a time, their father and stepmother had decided it was time for him to retire from the military and move back to Gbarnga and begin a small family business. They believed it was time to spend the rest of their lives together working in the church and serving the Lord. So, they started preparing for his retirement ahead of time. He saved some money aside at home and with one of his good friends who had a building material business in Monrovia. The plan was for Kerkula to take the suitcases back home ahead of his parents had the war not reached Gbarnga or Harbel.

MIRACLES IN THE SUNSHINE

During the incursion, the rebels associated the name Sirleaf mostly with the Mandingo tribal group, which was one of the two tribal groups they had targeted initially as enemies. The name Sirleaf is not limited only to the Mandingo tribe. The name is also found among the Via, Mende, Gola, Kpelle, and Lorma tribes. This is true even up to this date. Innocent lives were destroyed during the incursion just because they bore the name Sirleaf and other names that were associated with other tribal groups. Ironically, even some of the fighters within the rank and file of those who had specific connections to top leadership within the movement bore some of the identical names other Liberians used whom they had targeted, molested, and murdered. Interestingly, they spared the lives of those individuals but murdered the defenseless and innocent civilians. One can only wonder what kind of world we live in!

Preparing for the unknown, Kerkula had asked his brothers to throw all papers and IDs bearing the name Sirleaf under the sleeping beds in the kids' room. This was meant to prevent easy access by the rebels if they had come in the house. He immediately changed each person's last name from Sirleaf to Kerkula, a name that is still common among the Kpelle tribe. The change of names was purposely intended to protect the family from future harassments, intimidations, torture, or possible murder in the event the so-called freedom fighters confronted them. He picked the name Kerkula not because it was his name. He selected the name because it was familiar among the Kpelle tribe to which they belonged. Moreover, it was the first name of their late grandfather who was a dignified and famous traditional family man during his days in their village. Their grandfather's full legal name was Kerkula Gbatawei. He played a prominent role in the foundation and unification of their hometown, Mahwah, a small culturally conservative village along the St. Paul River that is mostly inhabited by members of the Kpelle, Via, and Gola tribes. On the other hand, the name Sirleaf is their family's name given to them by their ancestors who migrated from the Bopolu forest.

Long ago, the town of Mahwah was established by two brothers, Marvee and Seefeh Sirleaf, who originated from Bopolu in Gbarpolu County, Liberia. For decades, they lived, farmed, and raised their families in this town and have faithfully contributed to the socioeconomic development of Fumah District, Bong County, and Liberia as a country.

His father had gone to the window to see for himself what Kerkula had cautioned them was happening outside the house. He stood there at the window for a while looking at what was happening. He must have been bemused and in self-denial of what was occurring right in front of his eyes. He was neither sure nor convinced for a better word that the rebels were going to destroy any property or murder anyone. As stated initially, the management of Firestone had promised its employees and the entire plantation that there would be no murders, property destruction, or occupation of the plantation. Besides, being a commissioned officer and a morally minded individual, he thought it would be blatantly misleading and professionally out of character for a freedom fighter who claims he has come to protect and ensure the freedom of the "innocent" to begin killing the same innocent and destroying his or her properties. *Merriam-Webster* dictionary defines a freedom fighter as a person who takes part in a resistance movement against an oppressive political or social establishment.

His father questioned if the rebels were genuine freedom fighters after he looked through the window for a second time and saw two civilians wearing ordinary clothes being gunned down by a rebel a few yards away on the other side of the open field. He had always believed that the oath he took as a career soldier was in loyalty to the president of the Republic of Liberia and to defend the constitution, country, and its citizens against all foreign and domestic enemies. As far as he was concerned, Liberia was not in a political upheaval or under an oppressive political and social system that warranted a resistance movement such as rebel activities to remove a democratically elected government. He believed there were other nonviolent ways of removing a sitting president from office. For example, a president may be removed from office through an electoral process or impeachment proceedings rather than the barrels of guns.

His father believed the role of the military or any militant group is limited or subjected to the loyalty of the president, the defense of the constitution, country, and its people. He also believed that the "political wheel" of any nation could and should be turned by the people only through the process of elections and not warfare. He reminded himself that the scriptures say, "Put your sword back in its place,' Jesus said to him, 'for all who draws the sword will die by the sword' (Matt 26:52–53 NIV). For Kerkula's father, it meant that guns or any forms of weaponry should never be used to ascend to power or destabilize any nation or people. Ying-mao (1973, p. 180) had it right when he said, "War is the highest form of struggle for resolving contradictions, when they have developed to a certain stage, between classes, nations, states, or political groups, and it has existed ever since the emergence of private property and classes."

It became crystal clear that the rebels were heading to their house after all that had happened across the open field from them. Kerkula hurried to his father's bedroom and packed a small medical kit containing an asthma inhaler, peppermint candy, pain medications, a pack of bandages, and a flashlight. He gave the medical bag to his father and asked that he leave the house immediately and maneuver his way toward Bong Mines.

He said to his father, "The boys and I will be fine. Please make sure to take good care of yourself, and we will do likewise. By the grace of the Almighty God, we will find a way to get home to Bong Mines."

Kerkula knew if his father made his way to Bong Mines, he would have first saved his own life and second made way for his family to see him again. His father looked at him with a deep sense of perplexity on his face. He must have thought, "This kid is out of his mind to be ordering me around about my life and how to be safe. He must have forgotten that I have dealt with security issue for the past twenty-five year and most of my life."

The thoughts kept flowing through his father's mind as he stared right in his son's eyes. Kerkula did not relent but insisted that their father leave the house immediately. He listened to his son, grabbed the medical kit and walked through the back door. That was the last time in many months to come that they laid eyes on their father. It was also the last time that his father enjoyed the comfort of the house he once called home. As their father walked away, Kerkula turned to his stepmother and said, "Oldma [as they affectionately called her], the papay has left. We are not sure where he is going and how he will get there. I have asked him to do his very best to direct his movements toward Bong Mines, and we will do likewise. Hopefully, by God's grace, we will meet him there, or he will meet us there, whichever occurs first," Kerkula lamented.

She dropped her head softly as tears began to run down her cheeks on hearing what her son had just told her. Filled with mixed emotions, she was not sure what was going to happen to her husband, the man she'd loved so much and the one who had done so much for her. In her mind and from the expressions on her face, she might have been thinking, "Am I ever going to see him again? Is he going to be okay or are they going to find and kill him?"

Not only was she scared about the possibility of the rebels arresting and killing her beloved husband, but she was also worried about his health.

He often suffered from severe and long-lasting asthma attacks. That is why he carried asthma inhalers all the time.

The distress of all that was about to happen to her family, the fact of not knowing what was going to happen to her husband's life, and more left her stunned and perturbed. She was unable to contain the distress and therefore collapsed forcefully, descending toward the floor. Kerkula quickly reached out and grabbed his stepmother by both shoulders before she could even hit the hard cemented floor. He moved her onto the sofa in the living room and asked her to catch her breath before leaving the house. It took a few minutes before she regained consciousness.

By this time, the sounds of automatic machine guns and assault rifles began to intensify outside closer to their home. Surprisingly, something strange happened. God in his wisdom performed another miracle by confusing the rebels and caused them to wrongfully identify another building about two houses up the street as Kerkula's parents' home. "This is the commander's residence," one of the fighters screamed. Without delay, they pursued an aggressive attack on the other home but later realized they had made a mistake. They immediately turned to Kerkula's parents' home and began shooting and moving toward the building. By this time, everyone in the house, including Kerkula and his three brothers had already left the house.

Up to this day even when this book was written, Kerkula still doesn't know how this could have possibly happened. It must have been an act of God, another miracle in the sunshine for this to have occurred. The rebels were good at what they did and at carrying out reconnaissance missions. They were calculative in their plans of attack and in making sure mistakes were fewer than the successes they achieved. There were no possible ways that the rebels could have mistaken another house for his parents' house. Some in the family believed Tony must have been responsible for what happened. They think he may have misled the rebels into selecting the wrong house to give his family time to exit safely. Kerkula and his parents would like to believe otherwise. They think it was only by the grace of God and nothing else.

His sisters and their stepmother managed to slip through the back door unnoticed and went over to their aunt's house which was six houses up the street from their home. Kerkula and his brothers took the back road closer to the Catholic church and walked to the CQ residential areas for Firestone workers. The boys were forced to change their minds and joined their stepmother and sisters at their Aunt Matenneh's (Ma-ten-neh) home because

MIRACLES IN THE SUNSHINE

there was nowhere else in Harbel they could seek refuge. Moreover, they did not know where else to go or how to get out of Harbel to Bong Mines. It was Kerkula's first time in the city. Unfortunately, his brothers did not know where to go either or what way could lead them out of town toward Bong Mines. Their father always told them, "Know your environment so that one day when calamity occurs, you will be on the safe side of history." Once upon a time, their father also said, "In time of peace, be prepared for war." One could interpret it as making sure always to be prepared even when life seems pretty good, for no one knows tomorrow.

The Holy Scripture as recorded in John 9:4 remind us, "As long as it is day, we must do the works of him who sent me. Night is coming when no one can work" (NIV). Jesus' emphasis on work in relation to night and day is paramount to the effective use of time and the preparation of oneself for the unforeseen circumstances that are yet to come or could easily befall us individually or collectively. St. John also cautions us in chapter 10:10 that "the thief cometh not, but for to steal, and to kill, and to destroy, I am come that they might have life and that they might have it more abundantly" (KJV). John's caution in this verse is meant to remind us to stay alert and not be carried away or consumed by the activities of today because the enemy is busy hunting us.

It was evident that the boys did not pay attention to the words of wisdom their father had given them all these years. Reality finally set in and it seemed almost too late for them to figure out the meaning and importance of what their father always told them about time. They reached their aunt's house before the streets were finally cleared of the rebels' well-wishers and fanatics who had come out to celebrate their arrival. Everyone in the house including their aunt was happy to see them and to know that nothing had happened to the boys even though it had just been less than an hour since they separated from each other. Being overwhelmed by the enormous task of caring for the family and providing directions to them in the absence of their father, Kerkula moved to a secluded location closer to the window in the living room and sat down. He wanted to take some time to think through the situation and offer prayer to God for his guidance, direction, and strength to lead his family to safety.

Before his quiet time, he seemed very disturbed and worried about what could have happened to their father. Like his stepmother, he was troubled with mixed emotions. He did not know what to do or how he would have taken his little brothers safely to Bong Mines, the place they so desired to go.

49

A JOURNEY TO BONG MINES

Burdened by the situation, anxiety and frustration began to overcome him. He stood up and began to pace back and forth in the living room.

His stepmother called out to him from the kitchen, "Oldman [as he was affectionately called], sit down and get some rest, it will be alright. The 'papay' will be fine."

"Ok, Oldma!" he replied and went to sit down where he sat earlier.

As he got closer to the window, he decided to look outside and behold, what he saw will leave an indelible imprint in his mind that would stay with him for years to come and even up to this date.

From the angle where he stood at the window, he could see his father's house directly in the distance with a direct overlook of the open fields and the stairway. The stairway was usually his favorite part of the house to hang out. As he looked to catch a more unobstructed view of what was happening, he saw rebels on their bellies on the ground shooting intensely at his father's house. Pieces of shattered glass and curtain at the window could be seen flying in the air as the rebels intensified their assaults and got closer and closer to the house. Their next-door neighbors whom they met several years after the war informed them that on the day of the assault, there were rebels on every side of the house. They had surrounded the house to prevent anyone from escaping. One neighbor told Kerkula that one of the insurgents became so upset when they finally entered the house and found no one at home. He started shooting randomly in the air and corridors because he was not going to receive the recognition for killing the army commander and his family anymore. The rebels may have discussed among themselves that the one who was successful in killing the army commander and his family may receive a special acknowledgment.

He bravely stood at the window and watched the rebels climb the stairs, the identical stairs where he sat the night before. He wondered what could have been had the family stayed in the house, and the rebels entered. Lots of imaginations and mental pictures traveled throughout his mind as he struggled to understand why God would allow such savage war to occur in a beautiful and peaceful country like Liberia. He could not come to grips with why men with guns would so violently come against peaceful and defenseless civilians in the way they did even with no resistance. Chills ran down his spine and goose bumps immediately covered his skin as the rebels burst open the front door, entered the house, and began to shout a slogan in the traditional dialect of the Gio tribe, *"San-ga-lay-go-wa."*

He did not understand what the words meant then and even up to this day. He realized that the fighters seemed to have repeated those words as they celebrated a nonresistant attack. Some Liberians who are associated with the tribal group believed the slogan *"San-ga-lay-go-wa"* is ritualistic and demonic. They believed it empowers those who spoke these words in celebration of the demonic force(s) which made them fearless and gave them the strength to overpower their so-called enemies. Others believed the slogan was spoken in defiance to the sitting president whom they were striving to overthrow; the one whom they despised and considered their worst enemy. There were some Liberians who also believed that the slogan was more than a defiance but sabotage to the leadership and military capabilities. They echoed the slogan whenever military attacks were imminent against them. In simple terms, the slogan meant "you come against us and fail; we come against you and win."

Kerkula became more frightened as the rebels continued their assault on his father's home. He knew it was just a matter of time before the insurgents would begin to search for them. He turned to his aunt and stepmother and said, "The boys and I are leaving now. We have to separate ourselves from all of you to avoid one capture and one murder of our family. We are headed toward Bong Mines. Please do your best to head the same way if you have to leave from here. Please make sure to take care of yourselves until we see again." Those were his last words to his stepmom and siblings before turning around and walking out the door with his brothers.

They slipped through the back door just like his stepmother and sisters had previously done when they left their home. They maneuvered their way through the narrow path behind the buildings which led beside one of the electrical grid installations which were used to supply electricity to the workers' units. They came down a grassy but steeply sandy road which led them directly toward MC, one of the residential quarters. It is not clear what the letters MC stood for, but it was the name of a residential quarter at the time. The route they took avoided many people from identifying them. As they began to walk between the residential units, Kerkula met one of his old classmates, Paul Yarkpazoua (Ya-kpa-zoua) to be specific. He and his brothers were sitting on their porch and having regular conversations. A sense of relief overcame Kerkula as sweat came running down his face, arms, and hands as though he had been jogging all day. He was overwhelmed with the task of taking his brothers to safety, but worst of all scared for not knowing where they were going. He always liked to know what he was doing and where he was going. You would be right if you said, he likes to have control or be in control of any situation. He always wanted to be sure of the decisions that he took and their outcomes.

Paul noticed his friend from a distance as he came closer and closer toward his apartment. When he fully recognized that it was his former classmate, he got off his seat, ran and threw his arms around him and said, "Where you are guys coming from and where are you going?"

"It's a long story!" Kerkula whispered. "But thank God almighty that I have at least seen someone that I know," Kerkula continued.

"Come in and have a seat," Paul invited his friend and his brothers into his apartment. "You guys can stay here with us for now until we see what will happen," Paul told them.

Kerkula and his brothers accepted the kind gesture of his friend and thanked him.

They tried to make themselves comfortable in their newly found protected home but struggled to do so because of all the uncertainties and vulnerability. Paul's apartment was on a busy alley where residents walked daily on their way to work, farm, and the marketplace. Students also walked through the alley to school while taxi drivers, bike riders, and motorcyclists went back and forth at high speed. Accidents frequently occurred along the pathway. Residents had to be on a constant lookout for moving objects to avoid being struck by one of them.

Upon the arrival of the rebels, they used the same pathway to go back and forth between the apartments in search of their so-called enemies. They drove in open pickups and beat-up sedans with all four doors torn off and at high speed as though the area was an open highway. They ruled the streets and seemed to have had no regard for the residents. They shouted, fired automatic machine guns in the air and sometimes between the apartments as though they were on the battlefront or a firing range. They steadily blew the horns of their vehicles as a strategy to frighten their enemies or anyone who opposed their presence and activities. They required that all young men stayed clear from indoor during the day. It was forbidden for young men to be inside the apartments hanging out while they were on patrol at least within the MC residential areas. They found that to be either disrespectful or in opposition to their presence. They always wanted to know who was in the area and what they were doing for the most part, especially during the day.

MIRACLES IN THE SUNSHINE

Kerkula instructed his brothers to follow every single request Paul made to them and to stay clear from the indoors. He asked them to stay away from smaller groups and to behave normal to avoid suspension or questioning by the fighters. The rebels would often question able-bodied men who were sitting in smaller groups talking when they were on patrols. It was ironic how they demanded residents to go about their daily lives one day but came back the next day and condemned what they had said the day before. Innocent residents, especially those who were scared and couldn't stomach the presence of the fighters suffered the consequence of a daily change of orders.

It was highly irregular that different individuals issued daily change of orders within the rank and file of the movement. Some days it appeared as though they were in a state of anarchy. There were many days when residents panicked and became confused about not knowing which order to take. Often it would appear as though Camp MC was under attack by the AFL and another day by the freedom fighters. The multiplicity of orders along with numerous small pockets of attacks in the area made some residents, including Paul, his brothers, Kerkula, and his brothers, fear that the city was becoming more unstable and unsafe. They quickly figured that the area would eventually come under massive attack over the next couple of days. Therefore, they began planning to leave town and head to Division #34.

Evening came and night fell. The sounds of gunfire and human movements disappeared as the earth found rest from the violence from previous days. Life seemed to have returned to normal as the day broke and the sun appeared on the northern horizon of the city. Harbel that was known by its residents and visitors alike for peace and tranquility seemed to have bounced back from its misery and chaos. Vehicles occupied with freedom fighters rolled down the same pathway but at an average speed. The absence of hostilities and random gunfire during the early hours of the morning made it almost believable that the violence and chaos which had often beset the community had finally come to an end. Some residents were tempted to celebrate their newly found freedom but became skeptical because there were no orders from those in charge to do so. At one point, Kerkula and his brothers contemplated returning to their home by the open fields. They'd decided to cancel their walk to Bong Mines.

On the other hand, Paul and his brothers felt similarly and even decided to abandon their plan to seek refuge on Division #34. However,

53

somewhere in the back of Kerkula's mind, he knew that the sudden peace they were experiencing was not permanent but for a season. Kerkula knew that the activities of rebel warfare could not suddenly come to an end. He believed something more terrible or disturbing was about to happen. He encouraged his brothers and friends to stay alert and not to abandon their plan to seek refuge in a different location.

Amazingly, Kerkula was not completely done talking with his friends when suddenly a militarized vehicle mounted with anti-artillery with fighting men surrounded with guns drove faster down the pathway. They started shooting in the air and positioning themselves around the different units. A couple of them entered the apartments while others stayed in tactical military positions as though an enemy was on site or an attack was imminent. At first, residents were confused and did not know what was happening until one of them shouted, "We will capture and kill him right here." He shouted again, "No retreat, no surrender!" At the sound of his voice, the other fighting men began to shout the battle slogan once again, "*San-ga-lay-go-wa! San-ga-lay-go-wa!*"

Panic immediately engulfed residents as the news of new unrest spread across the community like wildfire. For a moment, it seemed as though enemy forces had beleaguered Harbel. Some residents who had gone to the marketplace to shop for food and were returning home got caught up unaware in the unrest. Some individuals whom I would like to call "brave street strollers" were spreading rumors of what was going on. These were individuals who may not have had any regard for their lives. They were either connected to the fighters in some way or had to be in the streets to hustle and make ends meet. They frequent the roads, day and night, even during intensive gunfire. The fighters chased away one of the brave street strollers who attempted to loot. He stopped by Paul's apartment and said to us that the soldiers had received information about the military commander for Harbel. He stated that they had located the commander in the vicinity and were in high pursuit of him. They believed that they were closing on him and did not want him to escape. He said it was the reason why there were movements of fighters and cars along the streets and alleys.

At first, neither Kerkula nor any of his brothers heard what this "brave street stroller" had said. They were listening to the 1:00 p.m. BBC *Focus on Africa* news. The national radio reported that the rebels had captured the Robert International Airport (RIA) and were advancing to the capital city of Monrovia. Robin White was interviewing a spokesman

MIRACLES IN THE SUNSHINE

for the Rebel Movement on BBC *Focus on Africa*. Kerkula was fond of listening to this station before and during the civil war. It was his primary source of reliable information. He made most of his daily decisions, approximately 60 percent concerning his movement from one place to the next based on the news report.

The brave street stroller finally caught the attention of Kerkula and his brothers when he began to argue with Paul's little brother, Jacob, about what he had heard from the rebels concerning the military commander.

"What did you say?" Kerkula asked him.

"I was not talking to you. I was talking to this guy sitting here," he replied.

"*Mann*, stop playing! I am just asking about what you were saying previously about the military commander," Kerkula insisted.

"I told these guys that I heard those fighters between the houses saying that the army commander of Harbel was somewhere around and they were about to arrest and have him publicly executed," he explained.

Momentarily, Kerkula's eyes turned red, and his body began to tremble. He immediately began to sweat as though he was about to pass out. One of his brothers almost shouted in anger at what he heard, but Kerkula managed to redirect his rage by pushing him into Paul's bedroom without anyone noticing what had happened. The brave street stroller did not recognize Kerkula and his brothers. He probably did not know the boys were children of the military commander whom he was talking about. He went on and on talking negatively about how the rebels were going to arrest the commander, drag him out in public, and behead him in the presence of everyone. It was apparent that the "brave street stroller" was a fanatic of the fighters. On the other hand, Paul and Jacob, but not the other two brothers that were visiting with Paul, knew who Kerkula and his brothers were.

Gunfire suddenly erupted as more fighters moved toward the location where they had suspected their father to have been hiding. They believed he was hiding in the public restroom and had no means of escape. As was often the case, impatience and failure to follow commands correctly led one of the fighting men to fire his rocket-propelled grenade (RPG) at the public toilet, destroying the entire building flat to the ground. The effect of the RPG was so massive that it also destroyed a couple of zinc shacks bathrooms built within the same area next to the public toilet which was built with bricks. They waited for the dust to settle and went looking in the rubbles for the mortal remains of the late commander.

A JOURNEY TO BONG MINES

Unfortunately, they did not find his body in the rubble or anywhere else. Up to this date, no one knows what happened to the commander after the shooting. There are many theories about what may have occurred on that sun-shining day. There are some who believed there was absolutely no way that the commander was in the public toilet when the fighter fired the RPG. Others thought he must have escaped the area or was aided by someone to leave the vicinity before the arrival of the fighting men. There were others who believed he must have possessed some supernatural power like some of the rebels which enabled him to leave the community without being noticed. Whichever theory supports the mystery surrounding the commander; it is almost evident that if he survived after the shooting, it must have been another miracle of God performed in the sunshine.

Their father was well loved and a respected individual within Harbel. Almost everyone he interacted with knew and loved him, including the men he commanded, the management of Firestone, market women, school-going children, and even some of Firestone workers who worked directly on the farms. He was a practical, down-to-earth individual but a professional soldier. He took his job very seriously and made sure to conform to the duties and responsibilities of wearing the uniform of the Armed Forces of the Republic of Liberia. He discharged the duties of the office of the commanding officer of the platoon in Harbel diligently and impartially. He was always willing to make the ultimate sacrifice to ensure peace among his men first and among the civilian population. He also had a respectable and professional working relationship with the PPD that managed the preliminary security affairs of the plantation. Some residents called him "the People's Commander," "Right man," "Professional Soldier." Others borrowed the family's nickname, "Papay." He found time to be with his family but made dedicated efforts to interact and relate to community members who stopped by his house, saw him in the streets, or came around the open fields. The Holy Bible according to Proverbs 22:1 declares, "A good name is rather to be chosen than great riches, and loving favor rather than silver and gold" (KJV).

One may convincingly argue that Kerkula's father chose to do what Proverbs declared rather than demand authority and power as some in authority would have easily done. He lived a simple and meaningful life, first as a soldier and as a community member. Some residents of Harbel who crossed his paths during and after the war still seem to miss him very dearly. Some even believe to this date that there can be no replacement for

56

MIRACLES IN THE SUNSHINE

him. Some believe, no one will ever fill the role as a commander like he did unless by divine appointment or selection. There may have been some who did not like him as a person or as the leader of the military platoon in Harbel, but those who favored him seemingly outweighed those who dislike him or were opposed to his leadership.

Ask me how I know, and I would say his way of life and the testimonies of those he impacted speak volumes. Some residents of Harbel have expressed how much they missed him. You do not need to argue much or conduct any investigations to know how residents loved, cared for, and missed him. All you would need to do is say his name to an actual resident of Harbel, and you would instantly receive a quick, emotional, and genuine response. An actual resident of Harbel would be someone who lived and interacted with the "Papay" during his tenure as the military commander.

Part Two

CHAPTER FOUR

The Journey from 45 to Kakata

THE NIGHT WAS LONG and restless as Kerkula and his brothers struggled with not knowing the fate of their father. At one point, they believed the fighters killed him during the attack on the public restroom and his body was secretly removed and disposed of by someone. They also thought like others that there is no way their father would have come to such an area to seek refuge. Amid their thoughts, Kerkula's little brother, who was next in rank to him had a different notion about their father. Among his siblings, he was closer to their father and spent more time around him than anyone else. They had deep secrets and interests that were common to the two of them. Both individuals were members of the "Poro Society," a traditional informal educational training center which prepares young men on how to become good fathers and a better citizen in society. No one would quickly know what they knew and had in common unless one of them volunteered to talk about it.

Early the Next Morning

While darkness still covered the face of the earth, his little brother woke up and tried talking the other boys into leaving town. He assured them that their father was fine and not dead. He said, "I have hope that we will see him again, hopefully in Bong Mines." He convinced his brothers, and they decided to leave town but did not know how and which way to begin their journey. Once again, Kerkula reminded his brothers of something their father always told them when they met as a family during their leisure time. Their father always spoke in parables. One of his favorite parables was, "A road doesn't climb a tree; it has to lead to a place whether good or bad." In other words, don't be afraid of where you are going but be cautious and take the necessary precautions to avoid unfortunate situations for the road you are walking will take you somewhere. He also told them to follow a "group" or "group of people" whenever caught up in a situation and don't know what to do or where to go. He believed following a group of people especially during crisis or war may not necessarily be the wisest thing to do, but for the most part, it reduces the possibilities of being singled out or facing unforeseen circumstances alone or without any help.

There were two large groups of people leaving town that early morning due to the unrest from the previous night. Though there were other smaller pockets of individual families that were also leaving, it was difficult to tell precisely if the small groups of families were escapees or were ordinary plantation workers headed to work. As usual, a good percentage of Firestone workers consisted of the entire family: the father, mother, and children. Sometimes the household included extended families like first or second relatives who lived with them. It was a common daily practice that workers on the plantation went to work very early during the break of day. The perception was the earlier a worker started work, the more he or she would accomplish in a day. Besides, he or she would have reserved more energy from the cool morning hours of work that would eventually take him or her through the heat and blazing sunny hours in the afternoon when the desire for food and water are high and inescapable.

Living on the plantation and working for the company was the so-called decent thing to do for a family striving to become self-sufficient. Practically, there were no other jobs available to find at the time but to work on the plantation. However, some residents who were mobile and had connections, took employment outside the city in places like RIA, Monrovia, or with the Liberia Agriculture Company (LAC). Working longer hours from the morning to the evenings meant doing more work and expecting a better paycheck at the end of the month.

In some instances, it would require every member of a family to participate in the workforce to keep the wheels of the family continuously propelling. Even school-going kids had to find or get involved with some forms of employment on the plantation. They had to make their contributions to the upkeep of their individual families no matter how significant or insignificant their contributions may have been.

The boys decided to join the large group that was traveling to Division #24 with the hope of going through divisions #27, 32, and 34. The goal was to enter Kakata by way of Robert Bright's farm, which was approximately 25

THE JOURNEY FROM 45 TO KAKATA

kilometers away from the city center. Taking that route would bring the boys much closer to their desired destination. Kerkula and his brothers learned about this precise route to Kakata during one of their conversations with Paul and his brothers when they stay at his apartment.

They knew no one in the crowd and couldn't quickly tell if the group was traveling in the right direction they had hoped to go. At three separate times, Kerkula tried to initiate conversations with some of the displaced people along the way to solicit reliable information from them. He wanted to know exactly where the group was traveling, but he failed each time he tried. He was mindful on engaging individuals he could talk with and not randomly approach anyone. It was unsafe and probably self-endangering to speak to anyone at that time about your plans or where exactly you were traveling because you could have spoken with a fighter, a rebel fanatic, or rebel informer on reconnaissance unknowingly. Equally, you could have spoken with a jealous person or a snitch that could have made life miserable for you later during the journey. Staying with the people you knew or were comfortable with during the trip was undoubtedly the best proactive security measure anyone could have taken at the time to save his or her life and probably the life of a relative or friend.

The group maneuvered safely out of Harbel into Division #44 without experiencing any gunfire or anyone being arrested or killed. Along the routes, there were vehicles mounted with rebel fighters, but they did not stop or harass anyone. They were singing warfare songs, waving their guns in the air, and blowing the vehicle horns. They keep shouting, "We are the freedom fighters, down with Doe and hail to Ghankay, our Papay," as their vehicle drove with excessive speed along the dusty paths. Many times along the way, the group had to walk off the roads and into ditches or grassy places whenever a vehicle mounted with freedom fighters was approaching closer to them. They feared being run over by the upcoming vehicle.

The pathways which led through the divisions to the city of Kakata were narrow. Evidently, some of the drivers for the freedom fighters were not trained adequately or did not have the technical expertise to operate tactical military vehicles. Some didn't know how to drive a 4Runner pickup truck carrying fighters on every side, including the hood, side doors, truck bed, and on top of the roof. Some individuals, soldiers, and non-fighters were literally picked up from the streets and asked, ordered, or forcefully made to drive. The wreckages of several accidents were seen along the ways. Evidence of abandoned or burnt cars could be found on the city streets, at

63

A JOURNEY TO BONG MINES

residential buildings, business areas, and even in parking garages. Most of them were the result of reckless driving or the drivers' inability to control the vehicles while in operation. These descriptions of the fighters are in no way meant to demean or ridicule anyone of them, neither is it meant to preclude the glory and appreciations some Liberians had for them. Rather, the descriptions are meant to paint a true picture of the evidence found during those historic moments in Liberia's history.

There were not many activities going on in Division #44. There were few residents in town. Most of them had already fled to the bushes, left for their hometowns and villages, or were hiding inside the brick walls of Firestone residential units. Some may have fled earlier because they knew groups of people fleeing the fighting in Harbel were in route toward them. They did not want to be caught up in a rush. Few brave residents stayed in town with the hope that the war wouldn't have returned to their village. Some of them had already been recruited and were being used by the fighters as Community Defense Force (CDF) to protect their local communities.

Their stay in Division #44 was brief. Some members of the group stopped to get water to drink while others rushed to beg for food. Those who had money and could afford the price purchased some of the foods that were on sale outside the residential units. The prices of goods found along the roads and in local towns seemed to have skyrocketed as demand drastically increased while supply crumbled. It is clear during civil unrest, merchants take advantage of the situation to exploit others by hiking prices. It has a greater impact on those with larger families and even those who must work harder each day to make ends meet. Unfortunately, even during normalcy, the government is unable to control or regulate the price of goods on the market, how much more are they able to control or regulate prices during a civil war?

No one could afford to be left behind. Everyone kept up with the pace at which the group was moving to make sure they stayed in direct contact. Leaving the group or falling back was not the wisest thing to do during the journey. If you were found alone walking further behind the group with no one in sight and came in contact with a rebel or group of insurgents on foot or in a vehicle, it was likely that you could be stopped, interrogated, harassed, and depending on how they felt, you could be let go, conscripted, or possibly mistreated. Therefore, it was always a clever idea to form smaller pockets of friends within the groups who could look out for each other. The concept of creating small pockets of friends within the groups saved many lives during the civil war. Group members were sometimes brave enough to vouch for each other especially in life-and-death situations. Even though some Liberians considered the rebels as wicked and heartless individuals, others thought otherwise. Freedom fighters were also human beings and everyday Liberians. There were disciplined as well as undisciplined fighters. They were sometimes pressured to listen to appeals when they came from a group of people rather than from a single person. Often, it didn't matter who made the appeal and why. Above everything else, being with a group was one of the best ways to stay safe and alive during the war.

The Invisible Checkpoint

By now you might be wondering what is meant by an "invisible checkpoint" and why should there be one in the first place. While writing this book, I thought about what name or terminology I could possibly use to describe what happened between Division#26 and on the road which led to Robert Bright Farm where Kerkula and his brothers were stopped at gunpoint by unidentified gunmen a few yards away from an abandoned Firestone building along the dusty pathway. No name or terminology was suitable enough to describe this area rather than calling it an "invisible checkpoint."

The group gradually reduced or disintegrated in size as some people branched out on different roads leading to other divisions like 43 and 40 while others stopped in divisions 37 and 27 along the way to Kakata. One common disadvantage of being in a group during crisis has to do with the issue of fear, which has been described as "False Evidence Appearing Real" (Shapiro and Shapiro, 2010). People are often quick to become panicked and fear the worst is about to happen. When this begins to occur, and no one is willing to step up and redirect the focus of the group, breakups, unnecessary talks, and the developments of opinions and myths will become eminent and inevitable. It was exactly the case with this group.

There was small talk going on among the groups and opinions began to develop. Some members of the groups believed going through to Kakata directly on the dusty pathway was unsafe and a disaster waiting to happen. Being on an opened road alone or even in groups was a potential danger. Some believed that it was safe to stay on the roads leading from Division #34 since they were relatively peaceful and quiet, while others thought the direct opposite to both opinions. They believed spending more time at Division #34 to get enough rest was a silly idea because it was just a matter of time before the unrest would come knocking on their doors as it did to them in Harbel. They would once again be forced to have to flee. Additionally, some believed going to Kakata directly on the dusty pathway was the right thing to do but entering the city from byways or side ways was an uncalculated risk to take because they could have fallen into ambushes on the outskirts of the town.

For Kerkula and his brothers, the goal was to reach Bong Mines even if it cost them their individual lives. They had already gone through the byways and winding roads, withstood hunger, lost sleep, fought the fear of death, torture, and endured the scorching heat and blazing sun on their backs. They had hoped to one day reach Bong Mines and be reunited with their family especially to see their father once again. Nothing was too big to overpower them, strong to stop them, disastrous to deter them, or persuasive enough to change their minds from going directly toward Bong Mines. They mentally fixed their eyes and thoughts on Bong Mines, and no sporadic relief of fear or hunger was enough to change course.

The four brothers were left alone to continue their journey toward Kakata. Even though there were smaller pockets of individuals still along the same pathways, they were further behind the boys and not in sight. Kerkula and his brothers had walked for a while and seemed tired and hungry. He decided to allow his brothers to slow their pace of walking since they were a few kilometers away from Kakata. Moreover, one of his brothers appeared weak, tired, and was falling behind every now and then. Kerkula supposed he was becoming more and more dehydrated and hungry, but there was no food or water in sight. That's why it became increasingly critical that the boys made their way to Kakata before night fell.

As they journeyed along the road, the other boys took turns helping their weaker brother. Fortunately, they met a Firestone worker and his family who were on their way home from working on their local farm. They had with them cucumbers, garden eggs, roasted corn, and some dried meat, which they took from their farm. Kerkula approached the man and gave him some money for the cucumbers, roasted corn, and a piece of meat in return. The farmer was glad to have helped Kerkula and his brothers just as he was thankful to the farmer for his generosity.

They stopped along the road briefly for their brother to eat. He drank the water the farmer had given to him before purchasing the food items. They bade the farmer and his family goodbye and continued their journey toward Kakata. After not very long, they came up to a Firestone brick building that seemed abandoned. From a distance, one could not see the building because the trees had covered the rooftop and there was no movement of people to suggest life in the area.

Shockingly, as the boys got closer to the building, what seemed like a tiny wire, spread across the entire road from one end to the next, seemed to surface. The area was as quiet as the graveyard and fearful as though something mysterious and demonic lived in the area. The road under the trees was wet as though rain must have fallen the night before. There were lots of dried leaves in the ditch along the way that had been forced by the moving rainwater. The trees and the wind stood still like military men during the inspection of the guards. Everyone heard a whisper about fifteen feet away but did not know who whispered. Suddenly, two gunmen came running from behind the building that seemed abandoned and shouted three times, "Single file! Single file!" I say, "Single file." Fear grasped the boys, and they became perplexed and did not know what to do.

It was the first time for them to have heard the words "single file." As the boys struggled to compose themselves from the fear that suddenly engulfed them, the gunmen came running toward them and repeated the words, "Single file! I say, single file! Where are you going and from where are you coming?" one of the gunmen asked frantically.

At first, the boys were confused and did not know what the words "single file" meant. The other gunman instructed them to line up one behind the other. The boys quickly arranged themselves single file as they approached the single wired gate circumspectly. By then, the boys had come face-to-face with the true meaning of their newly found words "single file."

The gunman asked again, "Where are you going and where are you coming from?" Kerkula being the oldest among the boys spoke immediately in response to the gunman's question for fear of allowing any one of his younger brothers to give the wrong response which could have jeopardized their plan to reach Bong Mines in a timely manner. A wise response to give a freedom fighter when asked, "Where are you coming from and where are you going?" was to suggest the name of the closest town or village. Some believed when you give the name of a town or village further from the fighter's position, they would instantly begin to interrogate you. They were mostly interested in knowing what was happening in areas that they did not have easy access to or a constant flow of communications with. The fighter constantly interrogated escapees or internally displaced people to gather more information on current events occurring in other

A JOURNEY TO BONG MINES

areas. Gathering information from escapees and displaced people helped ensured a level of safety, control, and security for some freedom fighters that had zero access to communications.

The closer the gunmen came toward the boys, the more they could tell that there were some strange things about the two men. The fighters were in their early twenties, wearing regular clothing like the other freedom fighters. Both men carried AK-47 raffles with extra magazine capabilities and had traditional artifacts, like wild bird feathers, cow tails, seashells and teeth of animals connected by thread around their necks. Usually, most villagers wore traditional objects like such during traditional and cultural performances or festivals but not in the way the rebels wore them.

They had red pieces of cloths tied around their foreheads and at the tip of their guns just like the first freedom fighters in Harbel. One of the men had fresh blood on his pants, hands, and on the knife attached to his gun. At first, the boys thought they might have just killed an animal and were cleaning it in the back of the building, but there was no smoke or fire that they could see, at least from where they were standing, to suggest that the men had been processing the meat.

The boys finally arrived at the single wired "invisible checkpoint" in a single-file position. One of the gunmen moved closer toward the checkpoint while the other remained a few feet away in position with his finger on the trigger and his AK-47 raffle directly pointed toward the boys.

The gunman at the checkpoint asked the boys, "Why are you going to Kakata?"

"To stay at our aunt's house on Bong Mines Road and take care of it until she returns from the interior," Kerkula replied.

"Are you sure, you know where you are going?" the gunman asked again.

"Yes, we know!" Kerkula replied.

"Ok! But before I let you guys go, come here with me. I want you guys to do me a small favor," the gunman added.

They quietly walked behind him as he led them to another ditch a few feet down the road from where they were standing. It was apparent that the boys were headed to see and do the unthinkable. Before they reached the "invisible checkpoint," two of the brothers had inhaled a repugnant smell of something which seemed like fresh blood along the road, but because the area seemed gloomy and deserted, the boys paid less attention to the scent or its origin. The boys didn't know there was no

68

escape from the inhumane, diabolical, and graphic scene they were about to witness. Little did they know the sight of the incident would pollute their memories and change their lives forever.

An Unforgettable Scene

He brought them to the side of the road under the rubber trees. The area was a little dark and scary. A huge presence of what felt like demonic force surrounded the place. There were dried leaves on top of the dirt that had been dug up from the ditches to allow free flow of rainwater and to prevent a flood. Ironically, there were no leaves in the ditch but a beheaded human body. It seemed the man must have had a fierce struggle for his life before he was murdered. He was a middle-age man probably in his middle forties. He was naked with both arms stretched tightly by his rib cage and bounded behind his back with copper wires. The wires were tied so tightly that it gradually penetrated his skin and began to reach his blood vessels. He had been beheaded from the back of his neck straight through to his esophagus leaving only a tiny layer of the outer skin which kept the head still connected to his body. Without the small segment of the outer surface, his head would have most likely separated from his entire body. The scene was very gruesome, and the boys couldn't withstand seeing how indiscriminately and mercilessly another human being was brutally butchered.

"Here's the favor you boys will have to do," the gunman said with his gun pointed at them. "Take this body from here and carry it across the stream of water. Lay it between the rubber trees and not in the swamp," the gunman commanded. "No one is allowed to turn around or look back when you lay the body between the rubber trees. Anyone who is found looking behind will be shot on the spot without any delays," the gunman continued.

The boys picked up the dead man and took him across the stream as ordered by the fighter. The dead man's weight was hefty to carry. It seemed he must have weighed twice as more than when he was alive. There is an adage which says, "A dead man's weight is much more than a person alive." There are many arguments and theories about the issue of a dead man's weight. Duncan MacDougall, MD, of Haverhill, Massachusetts, propounded one of many notable cases in the early 1900s. MacDougall theorized after conducting two separate experiments on human beings and dogs that a human body loses 21 grams of bodily weight at the point of death. He believed that the weight loss is associated directly with the human soul which departs the body at the exhalation of the last breath. He later seemed to have contradicted his theory when he confirmed that at the death of a human being, it is evident that there would be a loss of three-fourths of an ounce. There have been many rebuttals to his theory. One of such rebuttals came from Masayoshi Ishida (2010) in which she outlined four essential points against MacDougall's theory.

1. The uncontrolled escape of moisture from bodies due to insensible perspiration has practically no effect on the conclusion of his experiment that there had been anomalous losses in the weight of his patients upon death.

2. The speculated effect of convection air currents on MacDougall's balance scales does not exist.

3. Vibrational disturbances caused by cardiac and breathing activities, which disappear after the death of the patients, have practically no effect if the change in weight upon death is in the tens of grams rather than a few grams.

4. The speculative tricky role of buoyant force of air on the body can be denied.

However, for the purpose of this book, I will limit the details at this level but will discuss this issue more in future writings.

The boys were in awe of knowing they were about to face the challenge of carrying another human being's lifeless body; something they had never done before or thought they would have ever done. They moved toward the dead man slowly but cautiously knowing that any attempts to resist the fighter's order would have either resulted in a similar consequence or severe bodily torture. Kerkula being the oldest of the boys decided that he and the other brother next in age to him would be responsible to carry the body from the front by holding onto the man's arms while the other two boys would carry his legs. After positioning themselves, the boys picked up the dead man's body with the gunman standing about three feet behind them.

It was evident that the man had been murdered not very long before the boys arrived at the checkpoint. Kerkula and his brothers could still feel the warmth under the man's arms as they attempted to lift his body from the ground. At one point, one of the boys couldn't withstand the challenge and almost puked. Kerkula had to quickly ask them to put the body down and rest for few minutes, pretending as though they were exhausted. He did that to prevent his younger brother from puking. He was not sure what action the gunman would have taken against him had he vomited.

He said to himself, "If these gunmen could kill this man whose body we're carrying for whatever crime he had committed, they could do likewise to him or his younger brothers." Therefore, he had to make sure to protect them every step of the way. Kerkula also knew that the journey ahead of them was equally as far as the miles they had already covered and there was no guarantee of protection or excuse for the simplest mistake made. Truthfully, evil transcends good when wicked and lawless individuals control the moral compass of society.

It took approximately twenty to thirty minutes for the boys to reach what would be considered the final resting place of the dead man. They had to stop and rest several times because the dead man's body was too heavy to carry all at once. The weight of the dead man felt as though the boys were carrying a five-hundred-pound person. Each time the boys stopped for a rest, the gunman became agitated and began to yell at them. They will then pick up the body and begin to go forward. At one point, the gunman became a little too upset and fired four rounds of gunshot into the rubber trees. It became apparent that he must have been troubled by having a dead body at his checkpoint and really wanted to dispose of it. Maybe, he knew that eventually the body would begin to decay and smell had it remained in the same position for days. Maybe, he had fear of being caught or interrogated by his superior officer if the body was located at his checkpoint.

Further into their journey after the boys left the invisible checkpoint, they learned that a commander within the rank and file of the rebel movement visited checkpoints, especially during the evening hours and he would discipline and sometimes publicly execute a comrade if he or she committed a wrongful act against peaceful civilians or another rebel fighter.

Kerkula and his brothers laid the body between two rubber trees in the opened rubber farm, turned around and walked away making sure no one looked back as the gunman had initially ordered them. They were not allowed even to wash their hands. Kerkula worried about his brothers' lives. He had hoped that none of his brothers would have to lose his life because of a silly mistake he could avoid. He was continually giving them signs and signals on how to respond to questions. He winked his eyes, moved specific parts of his body in response to questions the fighters asked his brothers and if needed jumped in and answered a question that he thought was incriminating or a form of entrapment against him or his brothers. He did all of this so that his brothers would answer any question appropriately and not fall in trouble with the rebels. For the most part, the rebels had zero tolerance for play and nonsense. One may say, at some point, they struggle with making sound decisions; hence, they settled for the obvious, which on most occasions had a fatal outcome. Remember, Kerkula had promised his parents that he would take care of his younger brothers with the hope of bringing all of them home to Bong Mines. So, they did not have to worry about them but take loving care of themselves.

The boys arrived safely back to the invisible checkpoint after what seemed like a ride to "hell and back."

The gunmen thanked them and said, "Be careful going to Kakata. We might hopefully see you there tomorrow."

Confused by the statement from the gunman but glad to be released, the boys thanked them and got on the final leg of their walk to Kakata. They walked as fast as they could without looking back. They wanted no memories of the place that brought them face-to-face with death.

Upon their departure from the checkpoint, Kerkula warned his brothers not to look back but keep on moving forward. He feared looking behind while leaving the checkpoint could incite the rebels to take another action against them. Unfortunately, there was no way of knowing what steps the fighters could have likely taken this time or what would be the outcome. Therefore, staying focused on the road ahead was the best option to take.

As they descended the first hill along the road, they made the first turn and came up to an opened path which headed directly toward Kakata. Kerkula peeped behind to make sure they were all cleared of the danger they had escaped. He realized that the invisible checkpoint was no longer in sight. Immediate relief from fear overcame the boys as they feebly caught their breaths. Kerkula tried to calm one of his younger brothers from crying; the same brother who had fallen behind due to fatigue and hunger. He was overwhelmed by all that they were going through and could not withstand the absence of their father. He cried profusely that his brother wondered about his safety. They also asked if he would complete the journey with them to Bong Mines without falling into trouble or losing his life. He had been crying repeatedly, on and off along the road, about their father. He was worried if their father would survive.

THE JOURNEY FROM 45 TO KAKATA

Approximately twenty minutes after they left the "invisible checkpoint," they came up to "Bright's Farm" a poultry farming facility owned by Mr. Robert Bright. The facility was located on Division 26 Road toward Kakata. Bright Farm was known for producing several breeds of layers, including the Golden Comet Hybrid, Rhode Island Red, and others which provided a massive quantity of raw eggs, which were sold in the local markets. The layers were also used to produce meat for the consumers' markets. Unfortunately, poultry farming in and around the country suffered financial and infrastructural setbacks as a result of widespread looting and destructions of Bright's farm and other poultry farms, including Sangai Farm in Suacoco, Bong County, and Wulki Farm in Careysburg, Montserrado County, and other poultry farming in and around the country. As a result, they struggled to keep their doors of operations opened (Admin, 2014).

The boys walked past Bright Farm with no intimidation or harassment from anyone because there were no fighters around the area. Bright Farm, which was once noted for attracting marketers from around the country who came to purchase raw eggs and fresh chicken by the dozen, looked like a cemetery or a deserted village. You could hardly find anyone, including civilians walking the farm. The residents who mostly made up the working population at the farm had fled to their respective villages or moved to other cities in search of safety. A few yards down the street from Bright Farm was another tiny wired checkpoint. From a distance, the boys could see rebel fighters standing around a small "palaver hut," which they used as their checkpoint. Unlike the invisible checkpoint along the way, the gate ahead was in the open and had a little more movement of people both civilians and rebel fighters. There were mothers who carried their children, some on their backs and others walked alongside the roads. They must have returned from the streets, most likely the local street markets where they had gone to purchase food items for their respective families.

As the boys moved closer to the checkpoint, to their most profound surprise, a teenager carrying an AK-47 across his chest came running up the road toward them. He repeated the same words that the boys first heard at the "invisible checkpoint": "Single file!" At this point, Kerkula and his brothers were familiar with the words and knew exactly what to do. The young rebel fighter must have been 4 feet 3 inches tall. He had on a large hat with feathers and a red piece of cloth tied to it, shower slippers on his feet, and a heavy army jacket that was almost three times his size. From all indications, this boy must have been between the ages of twelve and fourteen years. The

A JOURNEY TO BONG MINES

AK-47 around his chest had additional ammunition that weighted him and hung closer to the ground. At one point, it seemed he was dragging the gun on the ground but managed each time to lift it back up with his tiny hands.

"Single file, I say!" he repeated himself, pointing his gun at the boys as they came closer toward the checkpoint.

Once again, Kerkula positioned himself in front of his brothers and led them in a straight line, following the order from the young fighter. They walked into a palaver hut one at a time. Each of his three brothers was interrogated, passed the checkpoint inspection successfully, and permitted to enter Kakata freely. Unfortunately, Kerkula was held back by the chief interrogator (as they called him). He claimed Kerkula was a spy from the government troops because he had a book which had a piece of notebook paper and a pen in his back pocket. The interrogator claimed Kerkula was using the items to gather information on the activities of the freedom fighters. The book was a Bible commentary entitled *The Power of God to Heal*. It was written by Evangelist Kenneth Copeland.

Kerkula was a devoted reader of biblical literature and commentaries. He carried a book with him every time he had the opportunity to do so. He used the materials for reading pleasure. It was a way for him to stay in faith and keep his focus on God and not the things that were happening around him. His brothers and even his parents knew about his devotion to the word of God and his interest in learning more about it. Before the war, Kerkula participated in Bible correspondence with a couple of religious institutions in the United States of America including Kenneth Copeland and Billy Graham Evangelical Ministries. He also had written communications with individuals across the globe through a program called "Pen-pals or Pen-friends." He had pen-pals from the United States, UK, Magnolia, Tunisia, Tanzania, and Botswana. His exposure, correspondence with the outside world, and sincere devotion to the things of God may have been some of the reasons why he was not overwhelmed or scared whenever he experienced a situation or became the direct victim of it.

The fighters kept him at the checkpoint for a long time asking him several intimidating questions. Their reason for the intimidation was to force him to confess to information that he had no knowledge about or possessed. For approximately fifty minutes, he underwent what I would like to call mental torture and verbal harassment. They took turns asking him relevant questions at one point and a bunch of irrelevant questions for most of the interrogation. As usual, being in authority, some chose to

74

THE JOURNEY FROM 45 TO KAKATA

yell at him during the questioning while others decided to remain civil and professional. All through the process, though frightened, he stayed composed and focused on the interrogation. Never once was the interrogation directed to the reason why he was held back, the matters concerning religious literature and a pen.

They asked several questions about the government's positions and operations in other cities including Monrovia. He had no clue why they asked him such questions. At the inception of the interrogation, he felt that the fighters had come to learn the truth of him being the son of the military commander in Harbel based on the types of questions they'd asked him. Also, during the questioning, he thought about telling them exactly who he was but held back. He was not sure it was the right thing to do. He knew if he had shown any weakness or decided to compromise any of the questions they'd asked him, it would have been the fighters' justification to take the ultimate decision, which most likely meant death.

The fighters struggled with the decision to let Kerkula go since he had not said anything incriminating to convict him. They couldn't find a reason to hold him in detention. They had hoped, apparently, he would have said something incriminating about himself or others that would have forced them to act against him. For the younger fighters, letting Kerkula go was not an option. They wanted him to stay in detention till night fell so they could carry out their plans. No one knew what the plans were, but it was obvious that no other plans could have surpassed a plan to get rid of him. It almost seemed another miracle had happened in Kerkula's favor to have had adult fighters conduct his interrogation. It was evident if the young soldiers had conducted the investigation, Kerkula would have been one of those unrecorded statistics. The Bible puts it right as recorded in 1 Corinthians 10:13, "There has no temptation taken you but such as is common to man, but God is faithful, who will not suffer you to be tempted above what ye are able but will with the temptation also make a way to escape, that ye may be able to bear it" (KJV).

CHAPTER FIVE

Kakata Police Station

FINALLY, THE FIGHTERS ARRIVED at a consensus to let Kerkula go. Interestingly, they handed him his book and the pen; the same items for which detained, mentally tortured, and bombarded him with random questions. On his way out of the palaver hut, one of the younger fighters whispered to him, saying, "God blessed you! You were about to see what we were going to do with you tonight." Kerkula looked him in the face and did not say a word or do anything. All through the interrogations, Kerkula had hoped God would look down on him and come to his rescue once again. God surely kept his promise and rescued him just like he had expected. Though Kerkula was very much afraid for his life, he knew God did not bring them that far to let the rebels kill him for committing no wrong whatsoever. He was also apprehensive about what would have happened to his younger brothers had they murdered him. He was fully aware that his brothers depended on him for directions and protection; not physical protection but with his words of wisdom and just being there for them.

During Kerkula's interrogation, his brothers had walked a few yards away from the checkpoint and had stopped at a yellow house along the road. The fighters had ordered them to leave the palaver hut and checkpoint area at once or get arrested. They had to leave their older brother behind because no one could stand around the checkpoint if he or she was not there for any reason. It was a dangerous place to be around the checkpoint without permission, especially at the gate where they kept Kerkula. The boys had to walk away to avoid any trouble but stayed nearby to maintain visual contact with their brother. They pretended as though they lived in the area to prevent other fighters from asking questions or residents from being suspicious of them. Kerkula caught up with them at the yellow house

76

shortly upon his release. His brothers were eager to know what happened to him and what caused them to have released him.

"I don't know what caused them to change their minds and let me go," he replied. "They gave me a hard time by asking things I had no clue about," Kerkula said. "At one point, I thought something had happened to you guys because I could not see or hear anyone of you talking outside. I was tempted to make up a story and tell them something about myself or an event in Harbel so they could let me go, but something held me back," Kerkula continued.

"I am glad you did not do that," his brother next to him in rank muttered."

His brothers kept asking him more and more questions as they continued walking up the hill as though they didn't interrogate him enough. But he did not want to upset any one of them. Moreover, he believed answering their questions as they walked would either make them more conscious about the ills of war or help get their minds off all that was going on with them now.

They finally made their way to the top of the hill and reached the police station without any harassment from a fighter or interactions with civilians walking by. However, they had to pass the last checkpoint which was within the police station. It appears everyone who came into the city on foot or in a vehicle had to go through the police station checkpoint before being allowed to settle in or go through the town. He and his brothers were no exception; hence, they took turns to enter the police station for inspection just like everyone else. The inspection line into the station was long but moved fast. Nevertheless, there was still more human traffic in and out of the station which prevented the smooth movement of the line. There were some individuals standing in the corridor keeping company while they inspected and interrogated others.

There were constant movements of fighters in and out of the station as though it was a marketplace. Kerkula became bemused; he had not seen so many rebel fighters at once in such a tight little space as he noticed at the station. Some of the soldiers were communicating in English, while most of them spoke practically common languages or dialects. Some were well dressed in military uniforms while others wore casual clothes like some of the fighters the boys saw along the way. The sign on the walls read, "Police Station," but most of the inspectors within the station wore military uniforms.

A JOURNEY TO BONG MINES

It was seemingly challenging to distinguish between the police and the front-line fighters. It appeared there were no distinctions.

A Narrow Escape from Death

It was quarter to 10:00 a.m. when the boys finally entered the police station for their turn to be inspected and interviewed. The clock on the wall was not working correctly to confirm the time, even though it ticked occasionally. The boys heard a senior fighter who had come with five of his men to drop off so-called government sympathizers. He yelled the time to his men as his voice amplified the urgency for them to get out and head to the frontlines. "Frontlines" was another new word for the boys. They had not learned the meaning of the word because they never heard it being spoken or defined before. Kerkula knew the meaning of the word very well. He heard it the first time when his Peugeot 504 had stopped at the "Iron Gate" checkpoint in Gbarnga (Gban-ga) where he saw a pickup loaded with armed men who shouted, "No retreat! No surrender! Frontlines, here we come!" His reaction to the pronouncement of the word was normal as usual with no surprises, but his brothers were skeptical and thought something terrible was about to happen.

He put his younger brothers first before him making sure he gave each one of them support and advice as they led the way through the interview process. Each one went through the process successfully but him. Once again, it seemed the dark cloud of trouble and unexpected mayhem had not stopped. He was about to experience yet another troubling situation, which he did not expect would come to him or his brothers. They had thought it was all over when they finally left the dark shadows of the rubber trees and finally entered the blazing sunlight in the city. They were wrong; the worse part of their journey was about to unfold. Unfortunately, this too was about to happen to the same one who had suffered previous intimidations at the hands of the fighters.

"What is your name?" the fighter asked.

"My name is Kerkula," he replied.

"Why are you here?" he asked again.

"We were told by the soldiers outside to come into the station for an interview before going to where we are traveling," he answered.

"Where are you headed?" he continued.

KAKATA POLICE STATION

"We are going down the streets from here to our aunt's house on Bong Mines Road," he answered.

"Who is your aunt? What's her name and why are you going to her house?" he asked.

"Her name is aunty Matenneh. She is one of our father's youngest sisters. She had asked us to come and take care of the house until she returns from the interior," he replied.

"Did you say she is in the interior? Where is that?" he asked.

"We are from Mahwah, a town behind Bong Mines," he replied

He paused for a minute before asking his next set of questions when Kerkula said they were from Bong Mines. The name Bong Mines may have triggered memories he had about the city, or he may have just been distracted by a passerby or someone in the room. They positioned his desk in such a way that it gave a clear and direct view through the front door to the main street. The front door was always kept open due to the massive flow of human traffic in and out of the room. It was evident for the most part during his stay at the station.

"So, where are you coming from right now?" he continued with his questioning.

"We came from Harbel, Firestone, by way of Division 44," Kerkula replied.

"What happened in Harbel that caused you to leave and come here?" he asked.

"Nothing bad that I know about, we came here because our aunt asked us to come and look after her house until she returns from the interior," he replied.

Kerkula was smart and articulate in answering the questions posed to him by the fighter. He knew if he had changed his answers at any time during the interrogation, it may have caused him and probably his brothers more troubles. He may have probably learned how to answer the fighters' questions, no matter the pressure or tricks from his previous experiences and interactions with them. An adage reads, "Experience is a great teacher."

He stayed composed and always kept his eyes focused on the interrogator. Though he was beginning to worry once again about his younger brothers who were asked to leave the station, he made sure to show no sign of worries or fear. The interrogation suddenly took a different turn for the worse when another fighter abruptly pulled the Kenneth Copeland Bible commentary from his hands and began to look through it. The moment

79

he noticed a sheet in the book, he immediately exclaimed, "What do we have here?"

He asked a rhetorical question with a straight gaze in Kerkula's face.

"We have another one here! This man is a spy. He must be on a mission from the government troops," the fighter exclaimed vehemently, alarming the other soldiers in the room. "Lock him up, right now!" he shouted.

Being more confused than ever before, Kerkula became speechless, but found the strength to speak up once again in defense of his own life. At this point, he found himself again between a rock and the hard place. He was in another state of confusion, trying to save his life and worried about his younger brothers. By this time, the first interrogator became dumbfounded and said nothing whatsoever to his fellow fighter about the accusation leveraged against Kerkula. He sat behind his desk chewing on a piece of tree root that was assumed to be for medical purpose. It became apparent that the dark cloud that once hung over his life had suddenly returned. This time, it seemed like the end had come and there was no escape. It all happened quickly. Neither Kerkula nor his brothers thought there would have been any more problems because they were already in the city with many people around, but they were wrong.

Upon his command, two rebel fighters standing against the wall came up to Kerkula and forced him into the corridor. They ordered him to take off his clothes including his tennis shoes. He was only permitted to keep on his underwear. They pushed him into one of four rooms in the corridor which was a jail cell. There were two other male inmates already in the cell. Both men were butt naked and tied up from the back just like the dead man that the boys had disposed of at the "invisible checkpoint." Unlike the dead man, the two gentlemen with him in the room were tied loosely but strategically to avoid any escape or maneuvering.

The Cell

The cell was dark, and it stunk badly. The odor was such a fetor that he wanted to puke every time he inhaled the scent. Upon his arrival in the room, it was hard to tell who was already there. He could only tell how many individuals were in the room by the sound of their voices when they spoke. The room was as dark as the barrel of a gun. The only light which came in was from the ray of the sun shining outside. In one of the cells on the opposite side of the wall was a lady who cried throughout the time he

KAKATA POLICE STATION

was in detention. She was also naked and was wearing only underwear. She was tied so badly with both arms behind her back and chest pushed forward upwards. Her breasts were full and leaked breast milk continuously. She must have been a young baby mother who was still breastfeeding. No one knew the reason for her detention.

The men in Kerkula's cell including those in hers could do nothing to ease her pain. It was strongly forbidden by the fighters to help another detainee become more comfortable or attempt to break or escape detention. Death was the ultimate price for anyone who tried or violated the command. There was zero tolerance for those behind bars. Detainees at the police station were considered "walking dead." In other words, they would not survive imprisonment for prolonged periods but be executed eventually or sent to fight at the front lines.

The lady wouldn't stop crying just as her breasts wouldn't stop shooting up breast milk. She repeatedly screamed due to the severe pain she was undergoing. At one point, a fighter shot his pistol twice in the corridor to quiet her down, but she came right back up crying. She couldn't help it but cry so they could have mercy on her and adjust the tie. Unfortunately, not one of the fighters responded to her appeal for help. All the detainees could do was listened to the soldiers and others in the room as they celebrated at one time then argued among themselves at another time. Ironically, the detainees did not know any personal reasons for their detentions. They were not allowed to talk openly to each other while in the cell. The fighters demanded that the cells stayed quiet like a graveyard because a superior officer would visit the station anytime.

Whispering or body language were the only practical means of communication among them. One thing they had in common was all of them were partially naked. They all came to know about a piece of frightening news they had overheard the fighters discussed. They heard the soldiers talk about the arrival and mission of General Paul, the supposed "Death Squad" Commander. They said he came every day at 2:00 p.m. to clean up the cell by taking all detainees, especially those who were naked and considered enemies. He took them to the creekside to make his sacrifice. The sacrifice they were referring to was to have those detainees murdered and their bodies dumped in the creek.

The clock on the wall in the front office began to tick, and the detainees' worries increased. There were no ways to correctly tell the time of the day rather than imagine it. No one could offer to tell them the time even if

81

they asked. Kerkula was wise enough to associate the brightness of the sun ray to the time of the day, but it didn't do him or the other detainees any good. Knowing the time of the day may have alerted them as to the possible arrival time of General Paul; it did not change the situation.

He had learned from a conversation with his father how to figure out the time of the day by following the rising of the sun in the morning, to its going down in the evening. Even though his timing may not have been as accurate as the actual times; in most instances, his estimated times were within close range of the same. His uncle, a rice farmer, had also taught him how to use the gifts of nature to interpret or associate every day's life. He had taught him that before modernization became widely accepted, his ancestors depended solely on the tips of nature to survive and those lessons learned are still useful today.

He felt tempted at one point amid worrying about his life and his brothers to help adjust the wire on the arms of the lady who was tied. Unfortunately, the walls in the corridor were too far apart that he could barely reach across to the other side where she was locked up. She struggled to move closer to the iron bars in front of her cell door so that he could help her, but she couldn't get much closer. She was in so much pain that she couldn't move her body. Regrettably, she had to stay in the same position and continued to cry for help at the top of her lungs. Unfortunately, every sound of her voice practically fell on deaf ears. No one responded to her cry for help. Her voice became so loud and unbearable that it troubled the other detainees. Sadly, they couldn't do anything but feel sorry for her. Her naked body lay on the cold cement floor in agony for hours with tears running down her cheek continuously.

Amid all that was going on in the corridor, Kerkula began to worry. It seemed he was giving up on life knowing that 2:00 p.m. was coming up quickly and he had not heard anything from his brothers. He felt the end was near. He knew he had been falsely accused, detained, and was about to face death for something he did not say or do. As he pondered over his life and all that was about to happen to him and his brothers, he began to fall asleep.

Suddenly someone whispered in his ears. "Wake up little boy! It is not time to sleep," the voice sounded faintly.

At first, he thought it was an angel, or he was dreaming. But it wasn't any of the two things he had thought. It was one of the other detainees trying to keep him awake so he wouldn't have been taken by surprise, if something were to happen. He was an older gentleman who Kerkula first met upon arrival in the cell. The man quietly began to tell him his story and how he was falsely accused, arrested, and brought to jail because he had refused to allow fighters to enter his rice kitchen on his farm. So, they accused him of sabotage and storing food for enemy soldiers. He was kind to Kerkula and encouraged him not to give up so quickly. He reminded him that only God could allow anyone to harm or kill him.

He said,

"I have been here for three days now and have not been harmed or killed. I heard that General Paul was coming to take us away on the first day I arrived here. He has been here twice and gone, and I am still here," the man continued. "Maybe it is a miracle that I am still alive. Or maybe my time has not yet come," he concluded.

"God forbid!" Kerkula exclaimed. "Maybe that time would never come," Kerkula added quickly.

"If God who has kept me this long in here can protect my life, he might do the same for you," the man said. "But it is crucial for you to stay awake while in here so you can stay on top of things that are happening in and around this building," he cautioned Kerkula.

"Yes sir! I will make sure to stay awake," Kerkula replied.

The afternoon was approaching very quickly, and Kerkula had not heard anything from his brothers or received any word from the fighters concerning his release from detention. He had hoped that someone at the front desk would have talked to the soldiers on his behalf to set him free. Sadly, his hope seemed to dash away every time he listened to them talking. He knew his release from detention would have only been possible then through another miracle of God. He began to feel sad as time slipped away and the expected arrival of General Paul became inevitable. He fought to keep his weary eyes opened as he continued to keep track of time by looking at the ray of the sun as it descended toward the southern horizon. At one point he became frustrated knowing that he had done nothing wrong to be detained and oppressed. He felt life had not treated him fairly and that he did not deserve the humiliation he was going through.

He began to question God, "Why me? What have I done that you seem not to come to my rescue again?" He even thought about giving up completely since nothing seemed to be happening in his favor. Little did he know God who had brought him thus far was not willing to leave or forsake him. He was about to prove himself once again as omniscient and omnipresence. God had decided from all indications to stay with Kerkula and his brothers every step of the journey. Maybe God was testing his faith once again, or maybe he was teaching him a greater lesson about the power and stages of faith, especially having faith in troubling times like what he was experiencing. In Deuteronomy 31:6, the Bible cautioned that Christians should be strong and courageous. "Do not be afraid and terrified because of them, for the Lord your God goes with you; he will never leave you nor forsake you" (NIV).

Throughout his imprisonment, he questioned his faith and his relationship with God, but he did not give up knowing that God is a miracle-working God. He knew that God must have had a plan for him since nothing was being done or said about his detention. Sometimes, when nothing seems to be working well or going as desired, that's when it is good to be still, listen, and wait on God. In Psalm 46:10, the Bible reveals that God encourages us to "be still and know that he is God; he will be exalted among the nations, he will be exalted in the earth" (NIV).

It was now after 2:00 p.m. and General Paul had not arrived. Honestly, Kerkula was not too sure that another miracle in the sunshine would have saved him; but he kept on trusting and praying. Kerkula was under the impression that even his brothers had abandoned him. He did not believe he would see them again. It had been a while since they detained him. The chances for his brothers to still be around the area were slim.

Interestingly, his younger brother, who had always been there for him, had slipped outside the station and stood on the side of the building after he and the other two boys had completed their inspections and were asked to leave the station. He had refused to leave his older brother behind, especially in detention. He had overheard the fighters talking about General Paul coming at 2:00 p.m. to clear the cells of prisoners and take them to the creekside. He heard the soldiers compared the creekside to the "valley of dried bones" as recorded in Ezekiel chapter 37:1-28 (NIV). Immediately, something awoke a resistant spirit within him as he reflected on the promise he and his brothers made to each other. They'd promised each other not to leave the other person behind, no matter what. Therefore, he decided to take the risk to go in and speak to the fighters to let his brother go.

He managed to slip back into the building and stood against the wall somewhere in the back where he could hear and see what was going on. The fighters did not notice him quickly from where he was standing. Besides, it was hard to tell who was a fighter or a civilian except for those carrying guns, dressed in uniform, or wearing other war attire. He later gathered the courage to go up to the front desk to plead for the release of his brother knowing that time was not on their side. As he approached the front desk, one of the fighters recognized him and said, "I thought you have already been here before," pointing his finger at him.

"Yes, I have, but I came back to talk to you about something. May I please talk with you?" His younger brother asked the fighter for permission to come in his presence.

"Come up quickly and don't waste my time! What do you have to say?" the inspector at the desk asked.

"Please, I would like to talk with you about my brother who you have in one of the rooms over there, pointing his finger to the corridor," his younger brother said.

"Which room and what is his name?" the fighter asked.

"His name is Kerkula. He is my older brother," his brother replied.

"Kerkula? What does he look like and when did he come here?" the inspector asked again.

"He is talking about the boy who has on white underwear in the other room with the two gentlemen. He is the one who was here with a book, pen, and sheet. We call him the Reconnaissance Guy," another fighter added quickly.

"Oh! So that's your brother?" the inspector asked.

"Yes, he is!" his younger brother answered.

"You must not be afraid of death, coming back and asking for a 'death roll' detainee," the inspector said, loudly.

"My brother is a good man; he is not what you think he is. He is not a soldier. He is a Christian. Please, I beg you to let him go," his brother pleaded with the fighter.

"You must be losing your mind; you will need to get out of here immediately!" the inspector said with a frown on his face.

"I am begging you; my brother is innocent. We came here to stay at our aunt's house and take care of it and not to cause any trouble. He is a good man; please believe me," he pleaded with the inspector again and again.

"I will say it one more time, get out of here now and save your own life or else you too will be put in jail," the inspector cautioned his younger brother one last time before turning around in his seat. He reached down in a small bag next to his desk and took a hand full of dried peanuts and began to eat.

Afraid but not dissuaded, his younger brother was forced to leave the building once again and went outside. He went back out and stood in the same area he was prior to coming in the building. Unexpectedly, he was asked to leave the vicinity altogether. He walked across the streets from the police station where he could see directly into the building. He made sure to stay around to hopefully see his brother for the last time before he was taken away or if he could find someone that would be willing to help talk on his behalf.

The Arrival of General Anthony

The evening was coming quick. It had been almost five hours now since they detained him. He had been there without food to eat or water to drink. The two other boys had already gone ahead to their aunt's house on Bong Mines Road and had not returned to check on their brothers. These two boys were younger and afraid. They could not withstand the sight of torture or murder. They were willing to do anything to avoid a crisis or get away from a potential life-and-death situation like what their older brother was experiencing. They did not understand the significance of a true blood relationship; what it means to put one's life on the line to save his or her sibling.

In his distress, his younger brother thought to himself, "Maybe I should go home and come back tomorrow. Hopefully, nothing will happen to him, and I can start a new day well prepared to continue begging." The moment he decided to leave and go to their aunt's house, a white pickup truck with more fighters in the back pulled up before the station. At first, he thought the moment had come when his brother was about to be carried away to the creekside. It was shortly after 4:00 p.m. and anything was possible. Historically, some Liberians typically do not respect time. Therefore, the arrival of General Paul could have changed from 2:00 p.m. to 4:15 p.m. and it wouldn't matter to anyone because he was the boss. No one dared say anything to him or ask him any questions about his late arrival. He was the absolute "man-in-charge" from what it seemed like at the time.

He hurried across the main street toward the police station but stood at a distance to hear the name of the commander who had just arrived at the station. Usually, the lower ranking fighters would greet their superior by saluting, mentioning a rank or calling his or her name when they come into their presence. His younger brother tried to seize the opportunity to know precisely who the commander was in the pickup truck. Asking others around for the name of the commander may seem a little suspicious, and he did not want to create more problems or suspicion about him. He had not seen or heard General Paul speak before. Therefore, he couldn't tell if the commander was General Paul or not. As the commander began to disembark his vehicle, his men tactically jumped off the packed pickup truck and positioned themselves rightfully to accord him due respect and provide the necessary security to ensure his safety.

He was a young-looking man, dark-skinned, and tall. He was dressed beautifully in a camouflage uniform with a new pair of black military boots on his feet. He looked polite and seemed highly respected by his men and even the other fighters who were standing around. No one called his name as he began to ascend the stairs into the station. His younger brother was convinced now that the time for their brother had come and the commander was General Paul. Something struck his memory as he watched the young commander climb the stair into the station. His face looked familiar, but the boy could not tell if the commander knew him or not. It could have been an uncalculated risk for his younger brother to engage the commander with the mind-set that he knew him if he proved to be someone else or even General Paul. Such an uncalculated risk could be considered a plot against the commander and would have received a deadly response from him or his men.

He mustered the courage within him once again to face the "giant" and began walking toward the entrance which led into the inspector's office. The commander was standing before the inspector at the desk when he walked in. Suddenly, the inspector whom he had previously spoken with became upset when he saw Kerkula's younger brother standing in the room. He stood up from his seat and said, "You, pointing at his brother, come here! Arrest this man!" he commanded one of his fighters. It seems, you have 'DI' and are very stubborn, but I will teach you a lesson," the inspector said.

"I am sorry, boss! I did not mean to upset you or disrespect your authority. I just want to talk to the chief," his younger brother said.

"Shut up!" the inspector said. "One more word and you are finished!" the inspector continued. "Sit down here! I will teach you a lesson!" His eyes were lit and red like fire; his face distorted with rage as he paced back and forth behind his desk.

Kerkula's brother was not sure what had just happened. Even the commander was surprised by the actions of the inspector. His brother became confused about the letters "DI." He did not know the meaning of it. He tried to figure out the meaning of the letters, but intense pressure from the other fighters prevented him. He was forced to sit on the floor next to the inspector's desk. He soon learned that "DI" meant "different intentions." These two letters combined were often used by the fighters to justify any action including murder, torture, or conscription of innocent individuals by the rebel movement. The letters "DI" were rampantly used among the fighters as it was among civilians. Ordinary citizens began to use "DI" maliciously out of context to incriminate and destroy each other while others misused the letters to crack jokes. "DI" became a self-defined, self-explained, and most incriminating two-letter combination or word that had ever been used in the history of civil unrest in the Republic of Liberia.

The commander soon became interested in knowing what was going on after he heard Kerkula's younger brother talk about him, and he looked him in the face. The commander thought he had seen the boy before but couldn't come to grips about where he met him.

"Soldier, bring the boy here!" the Commander ordered the inspector.

"Yes sir!" the inspector replied.

"What is your name and why are you here?" the Commander asked.

He gave his name to the commander and told him about his brother being in detention.

"Why is he in detention and who put him there?" the Commander asked.

"I did, sir!" the inspector responded.

"What did he do?" the Commander asked.

"He is a spy, sir! He was on reconnaissance."

"We found evidence and arrested him?" the inspector replied. "What did you find? Bring them and let me see," the commander ordered.

Immediately, he pulled open his drawer and handed the Kenneth Copeland book along with the sheet and Bic pen to the commander.

"These are your evidence for your accusation of reconnaissance?" the commander asked.

"Yes sir, but he was also behaving strangely, which made us even more suspicious of him and decide to put him in detention," the inspector added.

"Behaving strangely, what do you mean?" the Commander asked, but the inspector did not respond.

"What is his name?" the Commander asked.

"Kerkula!" his brother replied quickly.

The commander seemed to have forgotten the reason for his trip to the station. He became even more interested in Kerkula's case as the conversation went on and wasn't concerned that it was getting late. He walked up to three fighters sitting on a bench against the wall and ordered them to stand up.

"Come and sit here," he ordered Kerkula's younger brother.

"Thank you, sir," his brother said.

Before he could have a seat, the commander asked, "Where are you from originally?"

"Harbel, Firestone," the boy replied.

"Is that where your parents are from?" the commander asked.

"No boss! tThey are from Bong Mines," the boy answered again.

"Have your parents lived anywhere else besides Harbel and Bong Mines?" the Commander asked.

"Yes, boss, our parents settled in Gbarnga, Bong County, after they left Sanniquelle, Nimba County in 1987," the boy replied.

At the mention of the name Sanniquelle, the room became quiet, and the expressions on the faces of some of the fighters including the commander looked different. Throughout this time, the commander was standing with his men at positions of readiness, and Kerkula's brother was seated on the bench. But at the mention of the name Sanniquelle, he walked up to the desk and sat on it and continued his questioning of the boy. The interrogation soon turned into a friendly conversation, and Kerkula's younger brother was becoming more comfortable talking with the commander. He couldn't believe that he could speak freely with such a powerful man who had the keys to life and death for practically everyone within the building including the inspector. By this time, the atmosphere in the room was calmed and friendly. The initial tension had dissipated entirely. Interestingly, Kerkula himself was awake all this time and listened to almost the entire conversation between the commander and his younger brother. He had gathered the courage to sit up and hear the moment he recognized his brother's voice in the room talking at first with the inspector and later with the commander.

The commander decided to ask the boy one more question before leaving the station. He said to him, "Which school in Sanniquelle did you and your brother attend?"

A JOURNEY TO BONG MINES

"My brother and I attended Martha Tubman Elementary School," he replied.

At the mention of the school's name, the commander asked his men to bring Kerkula out to him. He told them to give him his clothes, allow him to get dressed before coming out. Immediately, Kerkula was released and brought outside to the commander. The moment the commander laid eyes on him, he held his head in his hand as he struggled to hold back his tears. His eyes turned blood red, and he became speechless for a couple of minutes.

"What's your name?" the Commander asked looking straight into Kerkula's face.

"Kerkula!" he replied.

"Who is your father and what does he do?" the Commander asked.

He called their father's name and told the commander that he was once an active duty commissioned officer in the army.

The commander paused, looked at the two boys and asked, "Do you know me?"

Everyone in the room seemed surprised at the commander's question, including Kerkula and his brothers. "No boss! We don't know you," Kerkula answered.

The commander turned to his men and began to explain a story of who the boys were, who their father was and what he did for him and his family. The commander told the story of how he and Kerkula started 4th grade together at Martha Tubman Elementary School and how he helped him with his lesson throughout the 4th, 5th, and 6th grades.

"If this boy had not been there for me during those years, I wouldn't have completed elementary school, and my parents would have been angry with me. As for his father, he was not only helpful to my parents but residents of Sanniquelle and all citizens of Nimba County. He loved and treated our people with love and respect and was always there for us," the Commander said. "He adopted some of our brothers as his children, some of whom are fighting alongside us today. He helped save the lives of citizens of Nimba County during the 1985 Nimba Raid. He also had a daughter with one of our sisters whom he took as a wife years ago." Facing his men and the other fighters, he said, "These are good boys; they are part of our family. They are with us and not against us. You should be ashamed of yourselves trying to kill good and innocent people. No one dares touch or do them any harm."

Kerkula and his younger brother could not hold back their tears upon hearing all that the commander had to say about him and their father. The front of his T-shirt was drenched in tears as he fought to stop himself from crying. He cried so hard that even the commander and some of the fighters had teary eyes. The entire room was filled with mixed emotions. For some of the soldiers including the commander, it was a beautiful moment knowing that they had just saved two innocent lives that in some ways were part of their family. For others, it was only another operation that was overruled by a superior officer.

The commander introduced himself to the boys as General Anthony. He did not tell them his last name even up to the time he left them. Up to this date, the boys do not know why the general chose not to give them his full name. Kerkula remembered exactly his full name but decided also not to tell his brothers because he respected the fact that the general decided to keep his last name private. Kerkula suspected that the general may have kept his last name secret for security reasons. He began to reflect as the general was talking about him and their father. He vividly remembered how both became close during their days at Martha Tubman. He remembered how he helped the general with his lessons in social studies, civics, English, science, and math, which the general did not mention. He thought about how they would use their recess or lunch hours to go in an empty classroom and study using the blackboard. They would first go out during recess and buy "cala" (car-la), locally made bread with hot pepper sauce, and Kool-Aid before going to the classroom to study. They would eat the hot pepper and cala to give them energy and keep them awake to study their lessons. It was their weekly routine throughout the 4th, 5th, and 6th grades. Their friendship came to an end after Kerkula graduated and enrolled at Levi H. Martin Baptist Elementary and Junior High School in Sanquelle.

Before leaving the station, the general asked Kerkula and his brother to come with him so he could take them home to their aunt's place on Bong Mines Road. Both boys along with the general and his men walked out of the station together. They stepped out of the station onto a narrow walkway and started walking toward the main street. Suddenly, Kerkula's younger brother heard his name.

"Nana! Nana! We are still here," the voice sounded from behind as they were walking.

Kerkula quickly found out as he turned around and looked in the direction where the voice came from that it was the other boys who had disappeared for a while. They had gone to the back of the police station to stay away from all the chaos, unrest, and back-and-forth movements of people. They did not leave the police station. They had been there throughout their brother's detention.

By this time, the general and his men were still walking toward the road while Kerkula and his younger brother stayed a few feet behind to allow the other boys to catch up with them. The boys were excited to see Kerkula once again after a prolonged period of being in jail especially behind bars at a police station that was notoriously known for sending innocent people to their deaths without trials. This police station was also known for making unnecessary arrests of ordinary civilians and falsely accusing young men as enemy fighters.

The other boys became excited at seeing Kerkula, even though he was away for couple of hours; they were glad that he had safely come back to them. They immediately jumped on him, hugged him, and began to speak their native tongue as they praised God for saving his life. His eyes turned blood red as he fought back the tears from falling from his eyes and running down his cheeks. He still could not believe that God had performed yet another miracle in saving his life. He was glad to be out of bondage and to enjoy the beautiful sunshine, inhale and exhale the fresh air. He was so thrilled that he struggled to come to grips with another found freedom. To him, it was another blessing of God. He was convinced beyond doubts once again, that the God who brought him and his brothers thus far would not leave them to the "Egyptians" but would make way through the Red Sea for them to walk on.

They hurriedly joined the general and his men as they kept walking without the fighters noticing that Kerkula and his brother had fallen behind to await the other boys. Maybe, the general had no time to notice Kerkula's temporary absence because there were too many people in the streets and around him. After a short walk, they reached their aunt's house. The general and his men bade the boys goodbye and left. To this date, the boys have not seen or heard anything about the general or any of the men that were with him on that day.

CHAPTER SIX

Aunt Matenneh's Home

Aunt Matenneh's (Ma-ten-neh) house was one of the most beautiful homes built in the community in which she lived. There were a couple of mango and orange trees surrounding the house. In the front yard, there was a small patch of land which descended toward an extensive opened drainage system facing the main road to Bong Mines. She used the land space to make a local garden. She planted pepper, garden eggs (bitter balls), okra, onion, and other vegetables as substitutes or add-on for the produce she purchased daily from the local markets to prepare meals for her family.

Her garden was famous and well preserved. It lasted for a while and attracted neighbors and passersby, especially those walking along the car road. Neighbors who did not want to go to the local market to purchase just a single item would stop by Aunt Matenneh's garden to pick some of her vegetables with her permission. Because of its usefulness and well-preserved nature, some of the neighbors began to call it "Dry Rice Market Garden." Kerkula remembered when he first visited Bong Mines in the late 1980s; his aunt had this garden in the same place. Back then, it seemed she had experimented with the idea of growing local vegetables in that portion of her land. Initially, it was a small piece of land, but eventually, it became a sizeable piece of garden land and had a variety of vegetables and other fruits. She did not have to fence or protect the garden from animals because there were no animals around. However, she had to look out for neighbors or passersby who took advantage to steal vegetables due to the opened access to the garden.

The entire yard looked utterly different from when he had once visited the area. There were vacant and abandoned houses all around the neighborhood. Most of the residents in the community had already fled to their local towns or villages. Some went to their farms during the day and came

93

home in the early hours of the evening. They stayed indoors all through the night to either avoid being troubled or noticed. At night, the area seemed like a ghost town. You could yell a person's name in one area and hear the name echoed in the distance. You could practically roll an emptied can on the road and hear the tumbling motion from afar. Residents in the area seemed not to trust or interact well with each other unless there was some level of familiarity that existed between them. Everyone seemed skeptical of each other. The fear of interacting or being found hanging out with the wrong people overshadowed the liberty of peacefully coexisting in communities where the reasons to fear and isolate your fellow human being were becoming prevalent and a daily norm. Residents had no choice but to adapt to this new way of life to stay alive or free from harassments, intimidations, and false accusations.

His aunt's house had five bedrooms and one restroom on the inside with an additional toilet on the outside. It was located under an almond tree close to the west end of her lot. The house was situated on a half acre of land and built in a ranch design. It had white paint on both the outside and inside. The bedrooms and other sections of the house were painted in assorted colors. The reflection of dazzling colors on the walls of the five bedrooms showed her love of bright colors and was symbolic of her admiration for elegance. Living in his aunt's house was a challenge for him and his brothers. Though it appeared they had gained their freedom from the fighters, there were no guarantees that their newly found freedom in their aunt's house would have lasted any longer. Night after night and day after day, intimidations, harassments, and conscriptions of ordinary civilians were either witnessed or spoken about by other residents.

Sudden Disappearances

The sudden disappearance of community members, especially young men and women, was becoming more prevalent. As morning came, residents wondered who had gone missing. Some community members believed that individuals who were forced out of their homes at night were either made to assist the fighters in moving arms and ammunitions to the front lines or were brought into the police station for questioning because someone snitched on them. Some also thought that some residents, especially females, were brought in at night because the soldier wanted to have good times while others believed it was just a way by which the fighters exerted their authority or control over the different communities.

One night, Kerkula and his brothers became terrified when a pickup truck loaded with armed men drove up into their neighbors' yard about two houses down the street from their aunt's house. There were approximately five men in total excluding the driver. They went up to the neighbors' house and banged on the door demanding them to open it. Upon opening the door, the fighters forced their way into the home. After a couple of minutes, they returned outside with three of the neighbor boys and one daughter. They forced them in the back of the pickup and drove away. The boys could not fully recognize who the fighters were. It was dark, and you could hardly see anyone in the distance but listen to their voices. The boys were not too sure if the men were enemy fighters or the so-called freedom fighters.

For several days, no one saw or heard anything about the neighbors' sons and daughter. Panic suddenly engulfed the community as more residents left for their local villages, farms, or moved to other parts of the city which had more residents or security availability. Kerkula felt that the men who came at night and took their neighbors' kids away might have been men who knew them or must have been around their home before. He knew that someone must have snitched on the family for the fighters to have only gone to their home and no other homes within the neighborhood. Reflecting on the talk between his younger brother and General Anthony, he wondered what would have happened had someone pointed them out as being sons of a military officer. He feared he and his brothers were the next in line to suffer harassments. He sensed the dark cloud that once hung over them and made their lives so miserable was finding its way back. Hence a need to change location was probably an innovative idea to consider. It was often a smart idea to change location more frequently to avoid being noticed too often in one community. Equally, it was also a risky adventure to migrate from one area to the next. The fear of not being known and identified by fellow residents could raise a suspicion against you, which might warrant the fighters to have you arrested and brought in for questioning.

Kerkula contemplated the idea of leaving his aunt's house with his brothers and move into a furnished but abandoned home in the next community because it was available. He feared the community in which they lived was no longer a safe place to be. What he didn't know was abandoned houses at the time were time bombs waiting to explode. The fighters kept constant surveillance on such homes and arrested anyone who was intruding or committed a burglary. Kerkula would have made the silliest mistake of his life had he left his aunt's house. Fortunately, Nathaniel, aka "Nat," a young man born to the union of Sierra Leonean and Liberian parents whom the boys met at their aunt's house convinced them to stay, and they took his advice.

Nat was a quiet, friendly, and helpful gentleman. He was approximately 5 feet 9 inches tall and dark in complexion. He had long hands, dark hair, brown eyes, and a strange accent. He spoke in such a way that others made fun of him. No one seemed to take him seriously. It was easy to get along with him. Moreover, he seemed to smile more often than being frown-faced. It was clear that he was more of a Sierra Leonean heritage than a Liberian. He was related to the boys' aunt from his mother's side of the family. He joked and laughed a lot. It was fun hanging out with him. He too had his share of misfortunes and harassments. One evening after he had cooked potato greens and rice, he took time to tell the boys about his own experiences and what they needed to know to survive the war. He began to explain all that he had gone through before coming over to the house.

They looked up to him as a "big brother." He seemed to make sense of the day-to-day activities of all that was going on in and around the community. He loved the news and current events which he gathered from listening to a small AM/FM radio he carried with him most of the time. He was very mindful of how he carried his radio. He was always concerned that someone might either steal it or use power to demand it from him. He protected the radio as though it was one of his vital organs. No one, not even the boys could handle the radio without his exclusive permission. He repeatedly cautioned the boys not to take his radio without his permission. Everyone knew this about him. Some residents called him "The Radio or News Man." Residents depended on him for updates on what was happening in parts of the country and the neighborhoods.

The first night at their aunt's home appeared to have gone very well for the boys. It was one of the first nights in several months behind the "lines"— rebel-held territories—that the boys had enjoyed relative peace at the dinner table. Though they sat on the floor to eat their food, they felt at home as they gathered around the large enamel bowl full of white rice and meatless potato greens. Each one of them ate the food using his bare hand because there were no spoons in the entire house. They had to sit on the floor to avoid making noise or creating a lighted house which could eventually invite unwanted or uninvited guests. Periodically, when families were at the dining table, uninvited guests, most times, the fighters would appear and demand that the cooked food be given to them to eat. Usually, they claimed, they had come to deliver the country from an evil regime. They would also claim they needed to be fed first to "combat the enemy." Ironically, often, the same residents who provided them food to eat were often referred to as the so-called enemies. Sometimes, situations became invariably complicated and one could hardly deduce from the fighters' actions or reasoning when they instantaneously made sudden life-threatening decisions. Decisions made and actions taken were mostly dependant on the fighters' mood and not necessarily the evidence gathered in a given situation. In the event the cooked food had already been consumed before the fighters arrived, the residents would be made to cook extra food for their so-called protectors to have a meal to eat at their table or have the uncooked food confiscated.

It was getting closer to midnight as Nat continued to tell the boys about his experiences in the war and his reasons for staying in Kakata. They were all gathered in the living room. It was dark and quiet, so that one could even hear a needle drop. They had cut off the lantern to avoid light from shining in the house, especially since it was late at night. The boys were not sleepy. They were having fun spending and enjoying the evening together, knowing that everyone had been well fed. They owed that wonderful stomach-filled night to Nat. He had worked so diligently to find and prepared food for them to eat. He made the ultimate sacrifice despite all that was happening during the morning hours in their neighborhood by going out to the garden, cutting potato greens and bringing them home to cook. The boys thanked Nat for his heroism in preparing food for them to eat.

There was a full moon and it shined so brightly. The boys depended on the bright-shining moonlight which penetrated through the cracks in the wooden windows of their aunt's house to illuminate the living room where they'd gathered. It was meant to avoid any light in the home at such a late hour of the night, which would have attracted or alarmed the fighters. They relied on the moonlight to at least see each others' faces and to navigate the house quietly without tripping on anything or making unnecessary noise. They stayed up very late through the night while enjoying each others' company. The temperature in the living room began to drop rapidly as the late-night breeze blew under the half-hung front door and cracked wooden windows. Darkness filled the atmosphere as the city slowly and quietly went to sleep. The boys were tired and could not continue with their night of fellowship any longer. Therefore, they decided to call it a night and go to bed. Two by two, they retired as a pair in their rooms, leaving Nat all by himself in the same position. He enjoyed sleeping in the living room instead of his bedroom. He felt sleeping in the bedroom put him at a disadvantage of knowing all that was happening in the entire house and the community. He believed sleeping in the living room would allow him not only the opportunity to see and know all that may quickly happen, but it could easily afford him many escape routes in case of eventualities.

Before the boys' arrival at their aunt's house, Nat always slept alone in the living room with no one else in the house. He felt even more secure having the boys around. However, Nat never forgot the atrocities he'd suffered which made him to always be on the alert as though something was about to happen. He always believed that if something had happened, it could happen again. Therefore, taking precaution and being alert were always mandatory positions to take especially during uncertainties. Approximately at 4:53 a.m., he heard lots of foot sounds and screaming on the outside of their house. The screaming was coming from the neighbor's yard whose house was located on the hillside just four houses from their house. The neighbor's house was built diagonally to their aunt's home, so that it became difficult for any one of the boys to exactly see what was going on. After not very long, the screaming turned into a loud noise and soon into a cry for help.

"Help us! Help us! Please come and help us; they are going to kill us!" The voices for help sounded loud and clear as they echoed between the houses into the dark.

Those were the voices of men, women, and children. As the cry for help intensified, a sudden outbreak of gunfire erupted and lasted for five to ten minutes. More men pulled into the area as the sounds of rushing vehicles could be heard coming in the distance. No one knew what was going on or what was about to happen. It was still dark as the moonlight had disappeared. By this time, Nat had gone into the bedrooms and woken the boys up. He wanted them to stay awake just in case they had to flee from the house. He seemed to have been terrified and was shaking as he tried to tell them about what had happened.

AUNT MATENNEH'S HOME

He told them, "Our community is no longer safe. This has happened in this area before, and it is probably going to happen again. Unfortunately, there is nothing we can do about it but to either live with it or move away."

Gunfire erupted for a second time and lasted approximately ten to fifteen minutes. News of a small cell of enemy fighters belonging to another warring faction who managed to slip into Kakata began to circulate in the community. It was assumed the enemy fighters forced their way into the local community and occupied one of the abandoned houses. Some resident believed that the neighbors who were arrested the night before were fully aware of the enemy fighters in the area but chose not to inform the authority. It turned out later the same day that the entire operation and harassment of the neighbors was a complete setup by the rebels to instill fear in the community and exert their control over residents of the area. At least that is what the boys learned after day broke and the incident had subsided. A similar event had occurred a couple of days after and was even more drastic than the previous. Some neighbors lost their lives and properties.

One elderly lady was instantly gunned down before her house by a stray bullet while sitting next to her small provisional table market during the earlier hours of the evening. According to the story, the elderly lady had just returned to relieve her grandson who had been sitting in for her at the market table while she went to complete her evening bath. The moment the boy got up and walked into his grandmother's house, he heard a big shake to the ground as though something substantial had fallen. He turned around and ran back to check on his grandmother, but she was not sitting in her bamboo chair where she usually sat. Instead, she was lying with her face down against the foot of the wooden table with blood running from the right side of her head. A stray bullet had hit her. The boy immediately collapsed to the floor when he noticed his grandmother was dead.

Upon regaining consciousness after his collapse, he cried so loud that the neighbors came to his rescue. Several days after, he visited the boys at their aunt's house and spent some time with them. He told them the entire story about his grandmother and how she had died from a stray bullet. To relieve his mind from what had happened to his grandmother, he invited the boys to come with him down to his garden to get some vegetables to prepare "dry rice" (an easily prepared dish in Liberia). He encouraged them to come quickly to avoid being seen by too many people. He knew that what had happened during the night was not completely over. He was under the impression that some fighters may come back to the area during the morning hours to make sure there were no unsolved issues or the presence of enemy fighters within the city. The militants were very good at securing control territories and protecting the communities under their control. They would always make sure to patrol the community back and forth to show their presence and made sure the residents knew they were still in control.

Part Three

CHAPTER SEVEN

The Journey to Bong Mines

FOR WEEKS, THEY HAD settled in and were becoming more comfortable living in their aunt's house in Kakata. They felt at home for the most part. They did not have to pay rent, utility bills, carry out house repairs or make any forms of payment to anyone, not even to a company. They didn't have to give their aunt any money for living in her house. All they had to do was keep the yard clean, find food to eat, maintain the vegetable garden, and stay safe and alive.

Their aunt had given them specific instructions to abandon the house and go to Bong Mines in case they encountered any eventualities or if the living conditions in Kakata became unbearable. They remembered the lessons their father had taught them growing up and the last conversations he kept with them in their living room in Harbel before leaving the city. Despite the lessons learned and the advice given to them, they knew the ultimate decision to either stay in Kakata or travel to Bong Mines rested on no one else but the four of them.

Kerkula was always mindful of making the right decision at the right time when it concerned his life and the lives and safety of his brothers. With Nat in the picture and living with them in the house, Kerkula knew he had to think a little bit more to make sure to include him and consider his wishes as well. It was the best way to ensure that everyone was on board with one plan and there were no other plans which could hinder their smooth departure from Kakata and eventually expose them to more scrutiny from the fighters. Exposing or making known one's departure from town to other residents of the community was an imprudent and risky decision to take. It created an opportunity for thieves and home burglars who were always on the watch for the last chance they had to break into abandoned or unlocked homes and steal.

103

A Ghost Town

Kerkula was not comfortable making decisions for the boys that included Nat. He didn't think it would have been the right thing to do; but he had to make them anyway because life in Kakata was becoming increasingly difficult. The garden they had depended on for the most part was running out of vegetables and greens. Neighbors and passersby began to visit the garden more frequently without permission. Even at some point, when someone was caught vandalizing or stealing crops from the garden, they would become defensive and often threaten to get into fights with the boys or Nat. There was a shortage of food in and around the city. One could hardly find local marketers in places where they used to sell. The city was becoming a ghost town as more and more community residents left town for their local villages. Word on the streets depicted the reason was due to the massive attack which was underway to the city of Monrovia with the intent to capture it and bring the war to an end. Security in Kakata was becoming fragile. Even though there was no curfew yet, residents were asked to stay off the streets especially during late night hours if they had no reasons for being there. They were asked to stay at home and conduct themselves accordingly.

At night, the city kept its silence as the moon began to shine in neighborhoods. Darkness soon engulfed the communities as the moonlight dissipated close to midnight. The power of darkness seems radiant as though the gathering of the "night gods" was imminent. The freedom fighters were the only men and women allowed in the streets at the time. They were on every street corner, security booths, and the main streets. It was obvious that anyone found roaming the streets at night was either a fighter, a fighter sympathizer or had some dealings with the movement and its cause. The night was a terrible time to be in the streets. It was practically difficult at times to tell who a true fighter or an enemy was. Being in the streets late at night meant you were exposed to some forms of danger, including but not limited to intense interrogations, harassment, torture, or imprisonment regardless if you had a reason or not for being there. There were not many considerations or second chances for those caught in the streets during the late-night hours. They were either treated as enemy fighters, individuals on reconnaissance, or thieves. Some, if not most of the "freedom fighters" especially in the ranks and leadership of the organization had zero tolerance for crimes and harassment of innocent civilians. Even though some people may think that the freedom fighter movement was pointless, intended to destroy innocent lives, properties, and demand unconstitutional power, there were some social and societal issues the movement initially stood to correct like the fight against sectionalism, nepotism, corruption, and bigotry.

Unfortunately, in the process of gaining prominence and fame among their fellow Liberians, the focus began to change. However, we were not surprised because we are reminded by the wisdom of Sun Tzu, who said, "All warfare is based on deception." Therefore, it is no doubt that those who plan wars have their personal motives and desires they wish to accomplish. Sadly, in the process of accomplishing their personal desires, others are deceived and often entrapped. It was evident during Liberia's civil crisis that those who fought and died the most were youth. The youth were and remain to this day the most victimized portion of our population.

According to a UNICEF report, more countries around the world are sucked into what is being termed as a "desolate moral vacuum" due to the increase of violence, warfare, and instabilities in these countries. "This is a space devoid of the most basic human values; a space in which children are exploited as soldiers; a space in which children are starved and exposed to extreme brutality. Such unregulated terror and violence speak of deliberate victimization. The continuation of this diabolical trend suggests there are few further depths to which humanity can sink" (UNICEF, 1996).

While it is true that an uprising without shared or common objectives is most likely considered unnecessary, some revolutions that are carried out against the so-called establishments or constitutional governments, especially African-led governments that refuse to relinquish "power" to the people when "power" is due, have their own sets of beliefs and justifications for beginning such uprisings. We may not personally agree with the rationale behind a rebellion, it behooves us by our citizenship to make sense of the underlined goals and objectives of any uprising which has the potential to impact us directly or indirectly as a nation and people. By doing so, it creates an opportunity for those of us on the fence to become problem solvers and not problem "pushers" or "deflectors" for lack of better words.

Kerkula was not a proponent of violence nor did he hold any radical positions against any constitutional authority, established governments, or leadership. He did not support the ideologies of any of the former warring factions in Liberia. He is a staunch believer of the undeniable truths of justice and equality, the protection of individual rights and freedom, and the absolute dignity of all human beings irrespective of tribe, county of origin, religious, political affiliations or socioeconomic status. Even though he did not support any of the warring factions in Liberia's civil crisis, as a Liberian, he's interested in the process whereby all Liberians can put aside their differences and work together for the common good of the country.

Some fighters exercised a high degree of moral compass, understood the principles of discipline, and a common respect for others. Periodically, they strived to protect residents in communities and did all they could to prevent or eradicate imminent threats and dangers. Equally, there were others who chose not to honor the values and aspirations of the leadership and what their movements stood for but to carry out indignations. Nevertheless, it is only fair to allow every man or woman to bear the consequence of his or her actions. The boys knew these facts about some of the fighters whom they interacted with before and during their stay at their aunt's home in Kakata.

Making the Final Decision

Nat, the newest member of the "flock" remained a constant concern for Kerkula in his decision-making process, especially regarding their stay in Kakata or departure to Bong Mines. He could not get the idea of making decisions for him off his mind, but he had to make one quickly because time was not on their side. Nat began to make erratic decisions about places he wanted to go, things he wanted to do, people he wanted to see and ideas of exploring new money-making ventures amid all that was going on in the community. Nat was somewhat territorial; he had managed his life single-handedly from the inception of the civil crisis when he fled his home leaving his parents, brothers, and sisters behind. He had been living alone for quite some time in Kakata without anyone's involvement in the decisions he made. Nat had to depend on his ingenuity to make decisions which allowed him to live out of fear while amid calamities that too often shaped his daily routines and threatened his life. He seemed unwilling to delegate or let anyone else have such authority over him. Nat trusted no one with his life but himself. He never took for granted the simplest mistake that had the potential of altering his life. Nat was very protective and continuously stayed on the alert. You may say, he was just scared, but one may argue that he was cautious and knew what he wanted to do with his life. He was not willing to settle for anything other than what was best for him and him alone.

It was still early in the evening hours, approximately around 9:00 p.m. GMT. The boys had just finished eating dinner and were gathered in their usual fellowship room in the living area. As usual, Nat was the entertainer or clown for the night as Kerkula would prefer to call him. He had a way of turning tense and fearful situations into funny moments. Nat was smart and cunning but highly argumentative. Nat would argue his point to the detriment of a healthy conversation. He was highly opinionated and came across somewhat unreasonable during casual conversations. Kerkula, on the other hand, liked to hold conversations, especially those that were meaningful and problem-solving in nature. Kerkula detested confrontations or the "blame game" which too often created sad and hard feelings among friends and even family members if not carefully monitored.

The evening started with one of the boys telling a folktale. His brothers considered him to be quiet and shy. Sieneh was not talkative but loved telling stories. You may say he was a traditionalist and a culturally minded individual. He grew up around his grandparents in their hometown of Mahwah (Mah-wah), a small town situated along the banks of the St. Paul River in Fumah District, Lower Bong County. Sieneh was fortunate to have received a rich traditional education while living with his grandparents and other relatives in their village. Kerkula could confidently say he was an expert in telling good and intriguing folk tales. His eloquence and tactics in telling stories were nothing less than captivating to his audience. Those who knew him before the war always referenced his unique abilities to mesmerize his audience during his storytelling moments. He was gifted and knew his ability to bring laughter and a form of traditional education by telling folktales to those who needed it the most. His story-telling ability almost created a rivalry between him and Nat.

Nat was not a fan of the "story-telling boy." He felt as though the boy told better stories than he. He did not like the idea that Kerkula often requested that the "story-telling boy" lead their fellowship time. He would often express his discontentment but couldn't do much about it but participate in the fellowship against his will. The "story-telling boy" soon lived up to his new nickname and forgot that he had a traditional name, "Sieneh" (See-nee), because his brothers became comfortable calling him by his new nickname and not by his traditional name. After not too long, some residents of the community began to call him by his nickname while others became increasingly interested in knowing how he got the name in the first place. There was not enough time for the "story-telling boy" to reveal to his neighbors how he received his new name and who gave it to him.

On the night of what would become their last fellowship time in their aunt's home, while the other boys were listening to the "story-telling boy" tell one of his best laughable stories, the sound of what seemed to be stray bullets flew through the roof of the building right above where the boys were seated. It frightened them, especially Nat and the "story-telling boy," who fell to the floor when he heard the first bullet ripped through the zinc. The boys became terrified and fled into their usual hiding place in their aunt's bedroom closet since it was spacious enough to accommodate all of them at once. There were small pockets of shooting lasting throughout the night until dawn. By daylight, rumors circulated that the massive attack on Monrovia to capture it and bring the war to an end was unsuccessful, and that government troops with the help of the West African Peace Keeping force were advancing on Kakata. A rumor was also circulated about enemy fighters belonging to another warring faction who were in route to Monrovia and Bushrod Island but were passing by way of Kakata. Also, there were others who alleged that some of those fighters had already infiltrated the city on reconnaissance and had been spotted and hunted down by "freedom fighters."

Tension and unrest gripped the city as more residents began to leave town. It was not too safe to leave the city during the early hours of the morning especially when going in groups. It created suspicion that would have led others to believe that one may have had information about a potential threat or plan on the city, which had prompted him or her to leave town abruptly.

As the day progressed, it became clear that the rumor about enemy fighters passing through town was a false alarm. Hence, the freedom fighters became more focused on the mission to Monrovia and not on the movements of ordinary civilians. The boys recognized the opportunity and took advantage to leave town as quickly as possible before the situation changed or became worse. Unfortunately, Nat refused to join them. He decided he was not going to Bong Mines but would stay alone at the house in Kakata as he had done before. The boys pleaded with him to come along, but he insisted. He claimed staying at their aunt's house in Kakata was the safest place to be rather than taking chances on the road to Bong Mines. Nat was not adventurous, he was an extrovert. He was skeptical about taking risks and tried to avoid any situation that he was not at least a hundred percent sure about. He believed in taking few and only well-calculated risks.

Kerkula knew that Kakata was no longer a haven for them, neither for Nat. He knew it was just a matter of time when some of the rumors would become truths. There is an adage which says, "To every smoke, there is a fire or something which has the potential of causing a fire." In other words, to everything that happens, there is a reason for it and to every rumor, there is some level of truth. Kerkula believed in this adage and considered seriously the probability of it becoming a reality. He vividly remembered many instances in his life when "smoking news" became real fires. Many flashback moments were going through his mind as he and the boys tried to persuade Nat not to stay alone in Kakata but to come with them to Bong Mines. One of such flashbacks that reminded him was the moment when his foster brother, Anthony, suddenly appeared at their father's home in Harbel and began to ask interesting questions. He gave them clues about some of the things that were about to happen, and they did come to pass. Though at the time Kerkula was bemused about what his foster brother told them, it was then that what he had said was beginning to make sense to him even more. The boys tried several times collectively to convince Nat to come with them, but he refused and insisted that they leave him alone and go on. So, they left him behind.

Let the Journey Begin

The sun was up early in the morning as the boys prepared mentally and physically for the long journey ahead of them. They knew that another chapter of their lives was about to unfold. They were more enthusiastic and excited about making this journey than any other walks they'd done before. The hope of finally reaching a place that they were more familiar with and a real part of their society was hours away. It was the day all of them looked forward to; a day when the promise made would have been a promise fulfilled. Even though the boys were saddened by Nat's refusal to come along with them to Bong Mines, nothing was mighty enough to abort their trip. It would take an act of God to change the minds of the boys from leaving Kakata on that day to Bong Mines.

The journey started at approximately 10:00 a.m. GMT. Kerkula and his brothers managed to slip away from the yard through a narrow pathway into a banana bush at the back of the house and onto the main road leading to Bong Mines. They'd maneuvered their way out of town without anyone noticing them except Nat, who knew about the plan. At the start of the walk, there were not many people on the roads, and the boys began to panic. Being on the streets alone, primarily all boys would raise lots of suspicions and concerns for rebel fighters. Some fighters might be concerned about enmity while others might be somewhat insecure and want to make sure that nothing improper or cataclysmic occurred within their controlled areas. One of the boys suggested that they walk through the bushes and not the main road to avoid upcoming vehicles or rebel fighters who were often found patrolling the streets. Kerkula insisted that they use the main road instead of the bushes to reach Bong Mines. He was aware that ambush was one of the rebels' tactics used frequently to attack and destroy their enemies. Hence, being in the bushes left an individual with little or no opportunity to distinguish him or her from an enemy fighter. To fall to an ambush put an individual at the disposal of the soldiers who sought to destroy their enemies. Being on the main roads did not guarantee the complete safety or freedom from interrogations or physical and verbal harassments. However, it created more visibility and avoided misrepresentations by the fighters. It also allowed the fighters to easily see and tell who was on the road at night or during the day.

Bong Mine is located approximately 33 km west of Kakata and 78 km northeast of Monrovia (Wilson, S.T.K., et al., 2017). The road to the city was not paved like many roads around the country. Because the roads were mostly gravel, the surrounding air was usually polluted with dried dust every time a vehicle passed by. The boys were always on the alert for strange noises, especially sounds of people talking in the distance or moving cars and machines. They would leave the roads and hide in the nearby bushes if a vehicle suspected of transporting freedom fighters was approaching them. Sometimes, they had no choice of leaving the roads when caught up in tight situations like being on a bridge or in a swampy area. They had to stay on the roads and brave the storm by facing the unexpected danger that was heading their way.

The boys had walked miles and miles away from Kakata hoping that the end was near. Unfortunately, the more miles they covered, the more it seemed the journey had just begun. Unlike the walk from Harbel to Kakata, the trip to Bong Mines was mostly peaceful except for a few situations along the road.

THE JOURNEY TO BONG MINES

The first situation occurred when the brothers had passed a man and his family headed from their farm during the early hours of the evening. One of the boys, the same boy who became tired, hungry, and kept falling behind during the walk from Harbel to Kakata, had asked his brothers to wait on him along the road while he used the bush to defecate. He walked down a small bushy pathway which led to puddles of muddy water about fifty feet away from the main gravel road where his brothers awaited him. His brothers couldn't see him in the distance but kept a normal conversation with him for safety reasons and to encourage him not to waste their travel time. He was notorious about disrespecting the value of time. His brothers knew this about him and decided they were not willing to take any chances by standing on the open road for a longer time.

In retrospect, the boys remembered it was the same brother who caused the delay during their walk from Harbel to Kakata and the lateness of their journey from Kakata to Bong Mines. They knew not to talk to him about his lack of respect for time and his disregard about their safety while on the journey to Bong Mines. They knew not to speak to him about it because it would have upset him and probably caused more tension among them. Kerkula, the self-proclaimed leader of the group, wanted to make sure that there was always peace and harmony among the boys. It was one way to ensure that the journey was successful and had no setbacks.

The second situation occurred when what seemed like a commercial vehicle with market women on board pulled up from behind the boys while they were walking. It was a red Toyota 4Runner pickup. The doors on each side of the pickup truck were either removed or destroyed on purpose. You could see through the vehicle from the driver to the passenger's side. There were a couple of freedom fighters in the back of the pickup truck along with few market women who were headed to Bong Mines from their normal market day in one of the local villages off the main gravel roads from Kakata. A gentleman seated next to the driver who happened to be the commander of the fighters in the pickup ordered the driver to pull next to Kerkula who was a few feet ahead of his brothers. Kerkula knew then they were in trouble and about to experience another setback.

"Where are you going?" the commander asked.

Before Kerkula could utter a word, four armed men with AK-47s jumped from the back of the pickup and ran toward the boys. One of the fighters grabbed Kerkula by the right arm, pulled him closer to him and asked, "Did you hear the chief? The CO [which stands for 'commanding officer'] asked you where you are going?"

"Yes, I did!" Kerkula replied. "I was about to say where we are going when you came up and pulled me," Kerkula continued.

"Who are you by the way and who do you think you are?" the fighter asked Kerkula with a steely gaze in his face.

"My name is Kerkula; my little brothers and I, are headed home to Bong Mines," Kerkula replied.

"Bong Mines! Are you from Bong Mines?" the fighter asked again.

"Yes, Bong Mines! We are Bong Miners, but we came from Kakata from our aunt's house," Kerkula replied.

"Shut up!" another gunman standing next to the pickup exclaimed. "These are the 'damn fools,' 'sons of a bitch' who were making the 'big money' in Bong Mines when the company was operating. I guess he ran away and now he is going back to find his money that he left behind," the fighter shouted.

Kerkula became bewildered and did not know what to say or do. By this time, the other two fighters who jumped from the back of the pickup were interrogating the other boys while the commander sat in his seat and watched speechlessly. Everyone else in the vehicle sat still and watched without saying or doing anything as if they were at the movie theater. No one said a word for at least ten minutes while Kerkula and his brothers were being verbally abused and interrogated. A preacher once said, "To every Pharaoh, there is a Joseph." You may not understand the meaning of this statement. However, it means to every lousy, wicked, heartless person or situation, there is a good person or a good outcome waiting to occur. Kerkula knew it was just a matter of time when the verbal abuse would have to come to an end. The scripture reminds us, "No temptation has overtaken a person except such as is common to man; but God who is faithful, who will not allow his children to be tempted beyond what he or she is able, but with the temptation will also make the way of escape, that he or she may be able to bear it" (1 Cor 10:13 NKJV).

The fighters kept harassing and intimidating the boys for more than thirty minutes, asking irrelevant and incriminating questions. Unexpectedly, one of the elderly mothers in the back of the pickup stood up and said, "I cannot take this anymore." She stepped out of the pickup and became vociferous. She appealed to the fighters to let the boys go. At one point, she was forced to tell a lie by claiming she knew the boys from their childhood days while growing up in Bong Mines. She propounded that both she and the boys' mother sold produce in the local market on John Hill and that often, she came with them to sell in other markets along the road to Kakata. "She is not feeling well today; that is why she decided not to come with us on this trip," the elder lady said to the fighters who were surprised by her sudden reaction. "However, I can take you to her house tonight when we get to Bong Mines so you may believe what I am saying to you," the elderly woman suggested emphatically. She became so firm and confident in her disposition that it claimed the attention of the CO, who left his seat for the first time and walked to the back of the pickup truck where they'd detained the boys.

"Let them go, soldiers!" the Commander ordered.

"Can they come with us since it is getting late and they still have a long way to go?" the older woman pleaded with the commander.

"This Oldma is full of it!" one of the fighters responded. "There is not enough space to take everyone. These are men; they will be fine."

"Let's go!" the commander ordered.

Disappointed and unable to convince the commander, the elderly woman stepped back up into the pickup, took her seat, and told the boys, "Be careful and do your best to walk a little faster because it is getting late."

At this time, Kerkula was glad that trouble had once again passed him and his brothers. He did not mind walking the rest of the way to Bong Mines whether day or night. All that he wanted was for him and his brothers to get to Bong Mines safely.

The evening was gradually falling, and the temperature began to drop. The shades of rubber and other trees along the roads made darkness appear much quicker. Kerkula knew if he and the boys had delayed along the busy Bong Mines roads, there would be no guarantees that God would send another "Joseph" to save them from another "Pharaoh." Therefore, he encouraged his brothers to hasten their steps to get to Bong Mines before darkness consumed the daylight. As they journeyed along the roads, every time they heard a sound of an upcoming vehicle or saw the lights in the distance, they hid in the bushes until the car drove past them. Kerkula was always the first to come out of the bushes onto the roads to make sure that it was safe for his brothers to come out and continue the journey. Sometimes, they had to stand in the bushes for a couple of minutes to make sure the moving vehicle did not stop ahead or was not reversing because someone had spotted a

A JOURNEY TO BONG MINES

person or something suspicious along the road. It was a dangerous journey, but they managed to pull through it successfully.

The boys had been on the roads for approximately seven to eight hours without food. They'd stayed long on the roads due to the stops and safety precautions they had to take to avoid problems with the fighters. As the sunlight slowly slipped away behind the dark evening clouds, the boys became hungry, tired, and thirsty for drinks of water. There were no homes or water wells open or available that they could go and get clean and safe drinking water. All they could find along the roads were creeks, streams, and still waters. It was not safe to drink from the rivers and streams along the roads. They were often dumping grounds for dead bodies, areas for defecations or laundry cleaning sites by the local inhabitants. Running streams and creeks were a little safer than still waters during desperate situations when water was most needed but hard to find.

Slowly but surely, they kept encouraging each other not to focus on the hunger for food, thirst for water or fatigue but how wonderful and pleasant it would be to finally reach the place called home. Further into the walk, the boys noticed from the distance what seemed to be beams of light in the clouds. First, they thought it was a moving object; probably a small airplane flying at night, one of the boys said. Another boy figured it could have been lightning in the sky or a light from a radio tower. However, it was not raining in Bong Mines that night, and it was not possible that an airplane could have been flying at that time of the evening. Since the rebels entered Kakata, Bong Mining Company slowed down many of its operations. Therefore, flying a plane during the late evening was a risk that the company couldn't have ever undertaken. It was a risk to do such a thing because the freedom fighters could have most likely considered it an enemy plane and shot it down instantly.

As the boys drew closer to the city, the excitement began to build up. They soon recognized some of the areas closer to Bong Mines. A boost of energy sparked a fire within each of them as they came to grips with knowing they had finally reached home. They entered the city of Nyian (Ny-ian) and noticed the haul truck tires still positioned on the right side of the road at the entrance of the residential area leading up to Rice Farm. It was a community within Bong Town which was home to mostly senior staff working for the company. It was also home to some of the entertainment centers, including a soccer field, tennis, golf, and bars. Momentarily, the boys felt good to be back in a community they were familiar with; even

THE JOURNEY TO BONG MINES

more delighted to know that there were family members and people they could run to in case of trouble. For Kerkula, he was not too familiar with Bong Mines like his brothers were. He had only been to Bong Mines once before the war to visit with his late uncle and his family. However, their father once informed them about family members, relatives, and friends who lived and worked with the company. Bong Mining Company played a pivotal role in the socioeconomic, education, and human resource developments of Fumah District residents.

At approximately 8:32 p.m. GMT, the wooden clock on the wall in their uncle's living room confirmed the time when the boys finally and safely arrived home. They were met upon arrival by their uncle and his wife, nieces and nephews, and other family members who were visiting from the interior. They cried together, hugged each other, and praised God for bringing them home safely. Their uncle was not a staunch Christian. He often did not practice his faith or make public confessions about it. Some family members believed he was a member of the Islamic faith and others thought he was a non-practicing, non-confessing Christian. There were others who also felt that he was an atheist. It didn't matter to the boys what religion their uncle belonged to, or the perceptions others had about him. They loved him for who he was. They knew him to be a good man and one of the best family members they had ever come to know.

He quickly turned their fatigue and weary looks on their faces into laughter. He was usually good at doing such with family members, friends, and most especially his children at home. He was good at telling jokes that made people laughed and even forget often time about situations they were going through. He told jokes about the boys' trip and what he supposedly thought would have been some of their encounters along the way as though he had experienced it himself or was there with them. Probably, it was his way of welcoming the boys at home and making them forget all that they had gone through all the days and nights they were on the roads.

He did not leave Bong Mines at any time during the war before the boys' arrival. He and his family left later when Bong Mines came under severe and continuous military attacks by another warring faction. At that time, life in Bong Mines became unbearable and unsustainable. There were no longer free movements of civilians but fighters. The only thing one could possibly think about then was to leave town and be safe. Unfortunately, the news about their uncle's death in the Ivory Coast reached each of the boys at separate times a couple of years after the war in Liberia had ended.

CHAPTER EIGHT

Bong Mining Company

Bong Mining Company (BMC) was one of the leading iron ore mining sectors in Liberia which produced a good percentage of the exported iron ore and other natural resources from Liberia to other countries around the world like Germany, Switzerland, Indonesia, Poland, and the United States. Liberia is among some of the leading countries in mineral resources with substantial iron ore, gold, and diamond deposits. Iron ore mining was previously undertaken by American and European companies in the areas of Bomi Hills. Bong Mines, Mano River, and Nimba (Wilson et al., 2017).

Between the years 1958 to 1965, BMC was established because of a bilateral concession agreement between the government of the Republic of Liberia and a German investment company for a period of seventy years. The concession gave rise to the establishment of the German Liberian Mining Company, DELIMCO. The establishment of DELIMCO gave the government of Liberia 50 percent of the profits in lieu of income taxes while the remaining 50 percent was owned by a consortium of German steel companies under the leadership of August Thyssen Hutte AG and 25 percent was given to the state-owned Italian steel company Finsider SPA. The management of DELIMCO was headed by E+B consulting services.

Bong Mining Company was one of four mining companies which operated in Liberia during the 1900s. Mining operations at BMC began in 1965 and became one of the largest mining operations of iron ore across sub-Saharan Africa. Bong Peak and Mount Zaweah were the two primary mountains initially identified for iron ore mining under the concession agreement. To date, mining operations of BMC in Liberia are still noted as the largest mining operations ever conducted on the continent of Africa.

The iron ore and other minerals extracted during mining operations by BMC were usually transported to the seaport of Monrovia by trains and

116

locomotives. The distance between Bong Range Mountains, the excavation point to Monrovia (which is the port of export), was approximately 80 kilometers. This distance was shorter and economically manageable unlike the distance from Mount Nimba, which was the excavation point to the port of Buchanan, which was the port of export. The distance from LAMCO to the Port of Buchanan was longer and approximately 260 kilometers. Iron ore and other raw minerals extracted from Mount Nimba were also transported by trains and locomotives.

Most of the mining operations of BMC were administratively managed from a central location. Like any other company or organization, there were other administrative oversights and operations in different locations that were supervised by senior managers and supervisors. However, the day-to-day administrations of the company were conducted at the Central Office. It was considered the administrative seat of BMC operations. Some residents as well as employees of BMC referred to Central Office as the "Powerhouse" because of the enormous management power held within this facility.

Central Office provided office space to top management staff, including the general manager (GM), heads of departments, senior managers, special contractors, etc. The management and administrative staff at this facility were responsible to conduct the day-to-day operations of BMC nationally and internationally. A representative from the government of Liberia was a part of the management team. He or she also served as a liaison between the government and BMC. The Honorable Theophilus Ernest Eastman, former minister of foreign affairs, Republic of Liberia, served as one of the last liaisons from the government to BMC before the civil war.

Present day—Bong Mining Hospital-Liberia

The Bong Mining Hospital was the only hospital in Fumah District, Bong County, during the war equipped medically to meet the healthcare needs of residents of BMC and other communities within the district. Apart from Phebe Hospital in Suakoko, Bong County, BMC hospital was one of the best within the country.

The construction of Bong Mining Hospital was part of the concession agreement between the government of Liberia and the German investors to meet the healthcare needs of the company's employees and their families. However, as the demand for quality healthcare services became increasingly high, the hospital opened its doors to the general public. Though this facility may not be operating at full capacity and standards currently, it continues to provide healthcare services to all Liberians and residents of Bong Mines. It remains one of the surviving landmarks of BMC.

Right exterior view of Holy Cross

This is Holy Cross Lutheran Church built by BMC in the early years of the company's operations. It was built purposely to meet the spiritual needs of employees and other residents of the community. It was initially built as a community worship center prior to it becoming the home of the Lutheran Church.

Sources close to the management of the church believe that the name, Holy Cross, was borrowed from a church in Dusseldorf, Germany. In 1972, Rev. John Kunkel, a Canadian clergyman, became the first pastor. John Amoah from Ghana served as an intern for a period under Rev. Berry Linh, another Canadian pastor. Rev. Thomas Z. Paye, a pastor of the Lutheran Church in Liberian (LCL), served as a visiting pastor during the transitional period after Rev. Linh's departure. Rev. Boima Yoko was later installed in the late 1980s as the first African to pastor the church after the missionaries.

Holy Cross billboard; erected after the war

Holy Cross Lutheran Church's billboard was constructed by the Women Auxiliary after the civil war. This billboard is in the front lawn closer to the road which passes before the church. Holy Cross Lutheran Church is a parish within Kakata District of the Lutheran Church in Liberia (LCL).

Back view of present-day Holy Cross

This is the present-day back view of Holy Cross. The basketball court in the photo was where the youth gathered to exercise and have fun sometimes after choir practices, Bible studies, meetings, etc.

Right exterior view of Holy Cross

This is a part of the exterior right front view of Holy Cross. The palaver hut in the rear was mostly used by the youth group during meetings, choir practices, discussions, youth celebrations, especially when it rained.

Front view of Holy Cross

This is the front view of Holy Cross with the driveway/walkway to the main edifice. The driveway/walkway leads directly to the car road in front of the church.

Driveway to Holy Cross (front view)

This is another front view of Holy Cross from a distance with the driveway/walkway to the main edifice.

Even though BMC no longer conducts mining operations in Liberia, it will always be remembered for the economic and human resource developments of the citizens of Fumah District, Bong County, and the Republic of Liberia. Up to this date, there are three institutional landmarks which will always reflect the presence of BMC: the church, hospital, and schools.

Although there were other unique institutions or establishments that can be associated prominently with BMC, including mining sites, the central office, residential neighborhoods, entertainment and business centers, and recreational facilities, these three landmarks previously listed will always stand out among everything else because of the significant impacts each had on the community and its people.

CHAPTER NINE

A New Life in Bong Mines

LIFE IN BONG MINES, for the most part, seemed to have remained at some degree of normalcy despite all that was happening to other towns, cities, and communities around the country. The city at least appeared to have been spared by God from the troubled civil war in Liberia. That was at least the first impressions the boys recognized during the first couple of days after they arrived. Day by day, the belief held by some Liberians that life would not easily return to normal in a country on the brink of civil war began to fade away as evidence of normalcy became visible.

Life in Bong Mines seemed to have proved wrong the perceptions of those Liberians who held the notion of normalcy not returning so quickly. The community seemed somewhat relatively calm. Bong Miners did not consider or expect the probability of another hostility erupting in or around the city. The leadership of BMC and the freedom fighter movement held bilateral agreements, and negotiations were kept professional and respected. The ability and willingness of both sides across the table to honor and respect the agreement reached helped to stabilize and build some level of trust between the parties and normalize residential living within the community. For the most part, both sides kept their obligations to the agreement. For example, BMC provided logistics, food, medical supplies, and treatments (availability of BMC Hospital) while the Freedom Fighters Movement provided security protection and ensured law and order. Arguably, some Bong Miners and other Liberians believed that the initial commitments to the agreement reached between BMC and the freedom fighter movement was better than other negotiations or agreements ever reached with any other investors during the period of the civil conflict.

Bong Miners are Liberians who have the audacity of hope and spirit of resilience, reliability, and unbrokenness. All through the civil crisis,

124

Bong Mines was considered a beacon of hope, a city of refuge and a haven for many who sought help and safety because they knew nowhere to go but run to the city away from the atrocities that besieged them. Residents were encouraged to go about their regular daily routines because of the signed agreements between the parties. Kids could be found playing in yards while others went to and from school. Buses drove freely through the streets conducting regular transportations of mine workers and other employees of BMC. Commercial transports and travels returned to some levels of normalcy as well. Farmers picked up their cutlasses as usual during the morning hours and headed to their farms while market women unpacked their produce (garden eggs, pepper, and okra) along with other dried goods in the local marketplaces. Stores along the streets of John Hill, Nyian, Cephas, and Varney's towns began to reopen their doors early after months of threats and rumors of war. Churchgoers attended Sunday morning services as usual while members of other religious groups went to their respective areas of worship.

The Church and Community

The Holy Cross Lutheran Church was one of two churches within BMC residential communities which attracted many Lutherans and other worshipers from in and out of the residential areas. BMC built the church initially as a community worship center where Christians from different denominations would peacefully gather and glorify God in oneness and the beauty of holiness. Bong Town High and Zaweata Junior High Schools built and operated by the company were academic learning institutions strategically established for the children and family members of BMC employees. However, some argued that the issue of class existed within the school system and unfortunately impacted enrollment, particularly into Bong Town High. They believed that the issue took preeminence over equal opportunity for all and hindered the pursuit of quality education by the less fortunate. Bong Town High School was considered the school for the elite children (general manager, assistant managers, senior managers, and superintendent) while Zaweata Junior High School was for the laborers' kids. Students from Zaweata Jr. High were not admitted to Bong Town High unless they had completed the 9th grade even though Bong Town High had accommodations at the same grade level.

Other enrollment opportunities to either school especially Bong Town High were seemingly possible if the parents of the student had some connections to the administration or it was based directly upon the student's immaculate academic credentials. Nevertheless, there were other qualified educational institutions within the public school system, including Bong Community High School, Christian T. Norman High School, JDK Baker Junior High School, and P. Lorpu Academy Junior High School, where students who did not receive admissions to either of the two BMC schools sought admissions. There is no information on whether BMC, Bong Educational System, and the Ministry of Education had any anti-class laws or policies on the books that prevented the denial of enrollment into any academic institutions within the country based on a student's class. Some believe that a law or policy of such nature did not exist in any of the school systems in the country because the issue had not been considered a national debate or concern even though it was becoming prevalent nationally.

The boys had finally made it home and were becoming acclimated to a new life in Bong Mines. Though it was the home of their forefathers, they had to make some needed living arrangements and adjustments to survive. The comfortable lives they had once lived in Gbarnga and Harbel were somewhat different from what they were about to experience. Their past had become history, and the challenges of the future were beginning to unfold. They had to prepare themselves mentally and emotionally for a new beginning to life which they had not experienced for many years. For example, one of the first challenges they had to face was finding comfortable accommodations and regular daily meals. Their Uncle Morris's home where they had sought refuge was jam-packed to capacity with family members and other relatives who had fled their homes from the civil crisis in other cities. There were no vacant rooms in the house for the boys to stay or enough food for everyone to eat daily. The boys had to sleep on the couch or spread flat sheets or whatever they were given on the bare floors to sleep on at night and remove them by day. Uncle Morris tried his hardest to accommodate and feed as many family members and relatives as he could, but stored resources (foods, waters, medications, cooking supplies, and ingredients) at home and the marketplace soon ran out.

Uncle Morris was a decent and high-spirited individual with a kind heart toward everyone. He treated everyone with love and respect regardless of who he or she was and what life they lived. He was gifted and had a good sense of humor. His charming persona always elated everyone in

A NEW LIFE IN BONG MINES

the room when he was present. His ability to make tense situations into meaningful and laughable moments was undeniably evident by the way he lived his life and interacted with everyone. It didn't take too long before you were embedded into Uncle Morris's contiguous jokes and fun play once you came in his presence. His family knew this about him. He was the younger brother of the boys' father.

Before coming to Bong Mines, the boys' father had spoken highly about their uncle. He used to love his little brother and admired him with immense pride and respect. The boys stayed at their uncle's house for a couple of weeks with their cousins, nieces, nephews, and other family members who they met upon their arrival. They had hoped life would have returned to normal faster than they were experiencing. They had also hoped that living conditions in other cities held under rebel control would have improved which would have encouraged their uncle's visitors to return home. It would have created more room for them to receive better accommodations and an increased portion of food daily.

Yes, indeed, life in Bong Mines remained practically stable unlike other cities around the country. Some Bong Miners referred to the stability of the city as "regular" or "good old days." The city seemed relatively peaceful and calm; business as usual went on but slower than normal. Kiss FM, the community radio station, continued to bring late-night hit music under the smooth operations of D. L. Porte, one of Kerkula's cousins. The African store in Benduma (Ben-du-ma) and Bong Rang Supermarket in Bong Town still had their doors open to the public. Club 63-CBR, the tennis court, and other recreational facilities were operating as well. Bong Town Community Hospital was actively receiving and discharging patients with no or limited exceptions for treatments. Throughout this period, it felt good to know that one could freely and easily cross the streets from John's Hill into Botota, Cephas town into Benduma, Nyian into the Main Gate and walk across the swamp from Botota to BMC Hospital for treatment or attend a regular church service at Holy Cross Lutheran Church. One could even go to the Central Office without any fear of being gunned down by stray bullet or by a freedom fighter if he or she was engaged in doing the right thing.

While they enjoyed relative peace and tranquility, the boys reached a decision that would break them up into two groups. They had safely arrived in Bong Mines, and it was now time for them to move on individually. Three of the boys decided to relocate to their hometown of Mahwah to engage in farming, hunting, and fishery to assist the older folks rather than being in Bong Mines. Kerkula stayed behind to help his uncle and to await the anticipated arrival of their father, mother, and other siblings. He went back and forth to Mahwah periodically to assist his brothers and to gather more food for his uncle's home. Soon, Kerkula began to make new friends and associated with others in his neighborhoods. He was becoming more familiar with his community and enjoyed the social interactions he was having with passersby who walked the streets leading up to BMC Hospital and in front of his uncle's home. He would sit on the front porch for hours each day when the weather was friendly hoping that his father, mom, or siblings would show up. He was optimistic that one day, they would all be gathered together in the same space just as it was in Harbel. He kept reminding himself that if God could save him and his brothers, he was surely going to save his father, mother, and other siblings.

Kerkula exercised his faith each day. He spent time praying for the safety of his family. Considering all odds, he knew only God had the power to save his family and to bring them home alive. He joined Holy Cross Lutheran Church and became a member of the youth group, choir, and the Lutheran Herald, a male chorus group formed by few young men within the church. He became actively involved in the youth group and held the position of secretary general under the dynamic leadership of N. Garpu (aka, "Uncle Nat" or "GAP"). Uncle Nat was one of many friends who would later shape the mind-set and leadership style of Kerkula when it came to work with young people, especially within the church or a Christian organization. Uncle Nat was brilliantly competent as a leader and witty in the word of God. He never gave up on plans that were established for the development of the youth group, whether it was at the Main Church or a preaching point. Under his leadership, no condition or situation was too big or hard enough to stop the implementation of any good plans that were developed to improve the youth. He was a steadfast, committed, and diligent leader. The entire youth group and church officials knew this about him.

The Trio

As living conditions gradually improved, Kerkula became more acclimated with the church's activities and Bong Mining community. He made additional friends, some of whom he cannot discuss in this book because of their privacy and relationships to other people. He eventually moved out of his uncle's home and took a room at a friend's parents' house. It was the

A NEW LIFE IN BONG MINES

beginning of what would eventually become a long-lasting friendship of three boys and one girl (Kerkula, Kenos, Jake, and Krubo—aka, Mamie). Mamie was the girlfriend of Kenos. It was in Jake's parents' home where Kerkula took a room. Many of their friends who knew the three boys referred to them as the "Trio." It was an unbreakable friendship which some of their friends believed was ordained by God.

The Trio lived, interacted, and supported each other in everything they did collectively or individually as though they were biological siblings or had known each other before the civil war. One would not eat without the others. Mamie was the biggest supporter of the boys. She made sure that the Trio had food to eat every day, soap to clean their clothes, provided medications whenever one of them fell ill, encouraged them to be in church on every Sunday and check up on them if a day passed by and they did not stop by her table in the local market place. She was a decent human being, polite, academically smart, family oriented, friendly, and above everything else, a hard-working businesswoman. The only concern anyone could ever give about Mamie was about being shy. She was not fond of many people. Occasionally, she would stay away from bigger groups of people but preferred to hang out with the boys any or every time the opportunity existed. I cannot emphasize it more; she was their biggest supporter and fan.

Life in Bong Mines had become enjoyable and rewarding, so that some Bong Miners easily forgot there was a civil war going on in the country. If you did not travel out of Bong Mines to other cities like Kakata, Harbel, or venture to Monrovia, you could not feel the drastic impacts of the war as experienced by some in other cities. At one point, Kerkula almost forgot that he had to make periodic visits to Mahwah to see his younger brothers and help the older folks. Convincingly, his newly found friends joined him during a couple of his trips to Mahwah. Soon, Uncle Nat became an unofficial member of the "Trio." Occasionally, they invited him to hang out with them during mealtimes, Bible study, holding meaningful discussions on open topics, recreational activities, or when they took a trip out of the city. You could depend on Uncle Nat at any time for guidance and maneuverability in any unforeseen situations. He remembered Kennedy told him a story about an unplanned trip he and Uncle Nat made across the St. Paul River behind Haindii during a period when security operations on the outskirts of the town were high. Freedom fighters were always on patrol and in small pockets of ambushes. It was not safe to be in such areas, particularly during the night hours.

According to Kennedy, he and Uncle Nat had gone across the St. Paul River to encourage the youth group in those areas despite all the insecurities and terror that were going on in and around the country. During their visit across the river, one of the youth members gave Uncle Nat a large pumpkin for his family. He brought the pumpkin with them upon their return from across the river. They stopped briefly at the local market in Haindii to purchase additional food and other items before heading to Bong Mines. Haindii is a town located on the banks of the St. Paul River approximately 8–9 miles (14–15 km) from Bong Mines. Occasionally, Uncle Nat would travel to Haindii on foot with a wheelbarrow on "market day" to visit the youth group. Upon his return to Bong Mines, he would stop and buy produce and gather firewood which he brought back to his family. The items he brought home would be used to sustain him and his family for the entire week until he returned to Haindii. Uncle Nat always knew his faith in God guided him. Throughout his journeys back and forth either to see the youth groups across the St. Paul River or in Haindii, he trusted God to lead him on all his walks even when it felt unsafe to travel. Uncle Nat knew his dependence on God was the only reason that kept him alive and safe. He also knew very well how to interact with people, especially the freedom fighters. He adopted a scripture that he carried mentally throughout the war. The scripture was this:

> I am sending you out like sheep among wolves. Therefore, be as shrewd as snakes and as innocent as doves. Be on your guard; you will be handed over to the local councils and be flogged in the synagogues. On my account, you will be brought before governors and kings as witnesses to them and the Gentiles. But when they arrest you, do not worry about what to say or how to say it. At that time, you will be given what to say, for it will not be you speaking, but the Spirit of your Father speaking through you. (Matt 10:16–20 NIV)

As a friend to Uncle Nat, Kerkula witnessed him practically use this scripture almost every day. It was virtually transparent that he knew the power of the scripture and how effective it was in protecting and saving his life. He was never shy to share the gospel with whoever he talked with or met. If they were willing to listen to him, he shared the good news.

Kenos also mentioned that he witnessed an interaction between Uncle Nat and a fighter that genuinely made him believe that depending on God's word was essential to everyday living, most especially, through the war. He remembered one night they had walked all evening from Haindii during one of their frequent trips and were feeling exhausted. They encountered the first fighter who had demanded that they open the market bag they had in the wheelbarrow. Uncle Nat informed the soldier that he was not going to open the bag because of its contents. The fighter insisted that he open the bag or expose its content either in the wheelbarrow or on the ground for him to see. Unwilling to endure the stress of going back and forth, he was forced to tell the fighter they were carrying a giant pumpkin which had been given to them by a youth across the St. Paul River.

At the mention of the word "pumpkin," the fighter became more concerned and asked, "Who are you by the way?" pointing his finger to Uncle Nat?"

"I am the president of all the Lutheran youth in this area, across St. Paul River, and in Bong Mines," Uncle Nat replied.

"Ok! If you're the youth president, then pray for us," the fighter demanded.

"No problem! I'll be glad to do so," Uncle Nat replied. "Before I proceed with praying can you please read a scripture for me?" Uncle Nat appealed kindly.

"Sure!" the fighter replied.

"Hand me your Bible, and I will read for you," he quickly replied.

He handed him a New International Version of the Holy Bible and asked him to read from Leviticus.

> Ye shall not steal, neither deal falsely, neither lie one to another. And ye shall not swear by my name falsely, neither shalt thou profane the name of thy God: I am the LORD. Thou shalt not defraud thy neighbor, neither rob him: the wages of him that is hired shall not abide with thee all night until the morning. (Lev 19:11–13 NIV)

At the end of the scripture reading, the fighter began to laugh hysterically about what he had read as though he knew what the reading was alluding to or what Uncle Nat was trying to get him to understand. He looked up at Uncle Nat and paused for a couple of minutes as though he wanted to say something. He smiled, shook his head, and asked him to pick up his wheelbarrow and go.

"No sir!" Uncle Nat replied. "I insist on offering a prayer for all of us before leaving," he continued.

A JOURNEY TO BONG MINES

The fighter was pleased with the offer and allowed him to pray. Immediately after the prayer, they shook hands with the soldier, picked up their wheelbarrow, and started their journey once again to Bong Mines.

During the civil crisis, there were some food items (e.g., pumpkin, lime, or kernel oil), behaviors (stealing, witchcraft, impersonation, womanizing), or clothing (e.g., wearing military uniforms or dressing like a freedom fighter) that ordinary civilians could not wear or bring around a soldier unless he or she was one of them. Foods like pumpkin, kernel oil, and lime were popularly known to be taboos to the fighters. Some believed that eating pumpkin, kernel oil, lime, or fooling around with any of such food items could instantly destroy or weaken whatever traditional or supernatural power the fighters had as a protection against their enemy.

After leaving the first freedom fighter along the road, Uncle Nat and Kenos walked throughout the afternoon and into the evening. It was getting dark and the temperature began to drop. Upon reaching the last gate on top of the hill in Nyeablah (Nyea-blah) on the outskirts of town just before entering Bong Mines, they encountered yet another roadblock. A fighter standing at a self-erected gate ordered the men to stop immediately. He was approximately a hundred feet away from where he had ordered them to stop. After a couple of minutes of adjusting his uniform and his boots, he picked up his AK-47 and ordered the men to come forward.

He asked, "Where are you coming from this late?"

"We went to Haindii to visit with our youth group and stopped at the local market and purchased some food items for our families," Uncle Nat replied.

"What do you have in your bag?" the fighter asked.

"Please don't give us a challenging time, sir. We just want to get home. We have been walking all day and feel tired. You don't want what we have in this bag." Uncle Nat responded.

"Don't tell me what to do! I will let you go when I decide!" the fighter responded harshly.

"Ma-man, we have things in this bag that belong to one of your generals, and I will let him know if you should take it from us. We have pumpkin in the bag, and I know that you don't eat it. That's why I don't want to open the bag," Uncle Nat said.

The fighter became concerned at the mention of a general's name and the word pumpkin. He released both men and asked them to leave his checkpoint immediately. Uncle Nat did not have food items in his bag for

132

A NEW LIFE IN BONG MINES

a general; neither did he know a general whose name he had mentioned to the fighter. Up to date, reflecting on that night, Uncle Nat still doesn't know how he came up with those words to the soldier. However, he knew that the scripture according to Matthew 10:16–20 must have come alive during his interactions with the fighter and it saved them.

Several months had passed, and life in Bong Mines was still relatively calm but deteriorating gradually. Security tension began to mount, and rumors of expected enemy attacks emanating from the Haindii area began to circulate all over the communities. A convoy of assorted vehicles mounted and fortified with armed men were spotted heading to the crossing point on the St. Paul River. Some freedom fighters believed that enemy fighters were attempting to seize and use the crossing point as a transport route for moving arms and ammunition, fighting men, goods, and services. The realization of an outbreak of war in Bong Mines was underestimated or overlooked by many residents including some management staff. It was assumed based on the agreement between the management of BMC and the freedom fighters movement that an attack on the city was unlikely given the fact that the security protection of the city had been entrusted to the freedom fighters and it had become their first and foremost obligation.

Before these new security developments, the record shows that BMC decided to dispatch the last batch of foreign workers overseas on the *MS Caspian Trader* through the Freeport of Monrovia on June 10, 1990. Before reaching this decision, BMC slowed down many of its operations. For example, the trains which transported iron ore, goods, and other services to and from the Freeport of Monrovia were no longer moving; primary mining operations were stopped or reduced toward the end of May 1990. The departure of BMC oversea workers gave rise to the arrival of the first group of freedom fighters in less than a month. However, the news about the freedom fighters movement and their plans to capture Bong Mines had been circulating long before the arrival of the actual fighting force. Some Bong Miners perceived that both the leadership of BMC and the movement were in constant negotiations before the arrival of the actual fighting force. They believed some freedom fighters may have even visited BMC community on reconnaissance long before their occupation of the city, which paved the way for a smooth transition of the fighting force.

Bong Miners were jubilant to receiving their freedom fighters as they were respectfully called and admired. Even though they had not experienced active rebel warfare within their city before, they were willing to

133

receive the fighters and live among them without expressing any sense of deep fear or pandemonium. Nevertheless, there were some like Kerkula and his brothers who had seen up front and experienced the presence and activities of the fighters. Somewhere in the back of his mind, it seemed too good to be true that the freedom fighters would have prevented or dismantled any enemy attack on the city without the destruction of properties and loss of civilian lives. He knew an attack by another warring faction would possibly result in the beginning of a new walk. He was aware that resistance to an army, a fighting force, or authority could either be internal—opposition from those within who oppose the presence of the fighters or authority; or external—resistance from outside the communities from those with different ideologies or the combination of both.

Close to the end of June, security alerts intensified as living conditions gradually declined. The fear of the unexpected was almost inevitable as more and more unwelcome news circulated the communities. Nevertheless, most Bong Miners hoped for the best and wished that the evil which beset them would pass over their city and not destroy it. Families that could afford to purchase additional food items began to stockpile their food pantries with more food, water, and other needed household supplies in preparation for what was yet to come. Those who could not afford to store up more food and other supplies in their homes decided to leave town eventually. Day after day, the streets were becoming isolated, and the marketplaces less populated.

The third interaction with Uncle Nat and Kenos occurred unfortunately but this time in Bong Mines and with a fighter who belonged to another warring faction. According to Kenos, he was sitting at home one evening relaxing when Uncle Nat came over and greeted him. At first, he thought Uncle Nat stopped by to keep his company as he usually did during the evening hours. Surprisingly, he requested that he accompany him to the church to pray and have some quiet time with the Lord. Uncle Nat sensed that the rumors of an attack on the city had spread far and wide and it had frightened members of the Christian community including members of their church (officers, lay leaders, and clergy) but most notably, the youth and young adults. He wanted to make sure to seek God's intervention in dispelling the fear which was rapidly spreading like wildfire throughout the communities and restore a sense of confidence in the word of God. Uncle Nat knew that prayer was the only way to banish that fear. As the leader of the youth, he formed a small praying group within

A NEW LIFE IN BONG MINES

the youth group soon after the war began in northern Liberia which was called "God Answers Prayer" (GAP). The group met weekly to pray for the protection of the church, its members, other churches, and the entire Bong Mining community.

Initially, Kenos did not want to go to the church with Uncle Nat. He feared the worst was going to happen to them. Besides, it had been previously announced on radio and in the community that a new warring faction had captured and taken control of BMC. Early in the day, they imposed a curfew, and everyone was asked to leave the streets. The fighter made an announcement that anyone found on the streets whether at night or during the day would be arrested and if necessary reprimanded for violating the curfew. Kenos reminded Uncle Nat that those were terrible times to be in the streets and he did not want to get arrested and reprimanded for his action. However, Uncle Nat convinced his young faith-minded friend by challenging his faith in God and appealing to him to come along to the church to make sure they prayed to God and checked on the status of a breadnut tree which the youth had planted in the yard of the church a couple of days before the arrival of the new rebel group.

The two men set up to go to Holy Cross as discussed. They walked through the deserted streets which led them to the church. Everyone was in their homes; not even cars or animals could be found moving around on the streets or in neighborhoods. The sun was shining bright, but the community was as quiet as a cemetery. Interestingly, the two men reached the church without any problems. They decided to go and see the breadnut tree first before entering the church to pray. They walked up to the youths' garden in the front yard closer to the main road and saw the breadnut tree. Before going into the church to pray, Uncle Nat decided to urinate. He walked up to the young bush next to the church, and as he began to urinate, a fighter who was blended well within the colors of the bushes stood up and put him at gunpoint. He was dressed up beautifully in his military camouflage and fully armed with a machine gun and ammunition strapped across his chest. He wore long dark boots on his feet and an army face cap on his head. His eyes were blood red, and he stood about 5 feet 8 inches tall.

Unlike other fighters, this fighter did not look fearful; he seemed to be a professional gunman. From all indications, it was clear that this fighter must have been on an ambush at the church for a while and may have even seen Uncle Nat and Kenos when they first arrived. Neither man noticed that the fighter was lying there. As usual, Uncle Nat seemed not to be frightened or afraid even with the gun pointed in his face. Unlike him, Kenos was terrified and began to tremble. He wished he had not gone with Uncle Nat to the church. Unfortunately, it was too late to think about what he could have done differently. He needed to stay focused on what to do to leave the presence of the fighter safely without any problems.

"What are you doing here? Don't you know there is a curfew, and no one is allowed to be in the streets?" the fighter asked.

"Yes sir, we know but you see, in times like these, we need God more than ever before. This is why we decided to come to the church and pray not only for ourselves but for our youth and for you good people who are protecting our freedom," Uncle Nat said to the fighter.

"Who are you?" the fighter asked.

"This is the second time I have been asked this question," Uncle Nat thought to himself. "I am the youth president of this church, and this is my brother," Uncle Nat replied.

"The both of you belong to this Church?" the fighter asked.

"Yes sir! We both are members of the youth group. You see, we have come here to pray for God to take away the fear from our church members, especially the youth. It would make them comfortable in coming to church on Sunday, attend youth meetings and Bible study knowing that we are in your capable hands," Uncle Nat replied.

"Do you have keys to the church?" the fighter asked.

"Yes sir! We do!" Uncle Nat responded.

At this point, Uncle Nat was the only one talking with the fighter. Kenos was still terrified and chose not to utter a word but allow Uncle Nat to handle the talking alone. He trusted Uncle Nat's ability to say the right words that would eventually set them free because he had done it before.

"Ok, if you do have the keys to the church come with me and open the door. You only have one try. The first key you put in the lock must open it, if not I will execute the two of you right here," the fighter added.

Kenos became more frightened and worried by what the fighter had said, but Uncle Nat stayed calmed as though their lives did not matter. They walked before the soldier and reached the main door to the church's entrance. Uncle Nat trusted that God did not bring them to the church just to be murdered by an unknown gunman. He knew that the God who had carried them throughout other situations would bring them through this one as well. Besides, he faithfully carried the bundle of keys with him to the church every day and used it every time it was needed. Uncle Nat was pretty much

A NEW LIFE IN BONG MINES

familiar with each key on the bundle and knew what doors they could easily open. He walked confidently to the front door, picked the right key from the bunch and inserted it in the lock. He turned the key counterclockwise, grabbed the handle and turned it also. Immediately, the door opened, and he invited the fighter and Kenos to come in and pray together, but the soldier insisted that he was fine and did not want to come in.

When the door opened at the first try of the key, the fighter was convinced that both men had told him the truth and there was nothing else to be done with them. He immediately moved back a couple of steps away from the doorway and asked the men to be cautious while at the church because they could come under another attack anytime. The fighter wished the men good luck, turned around and walked away. He vanished suddenly without a trace, and they never laid eyes on him again. Both men stayed at the church for a while praying and singing praise songs to God before leaving. They managed to make their way to a neighbor's home which was a few blocks away from the church and the main hospital. The neighbor was a staunch member of the church, and her daughters were members of the youth group. They knew both men very well and interacted with them often. Both Uncle Nat and Kenos stayed at the neighbor's home for a while until the situation calmed down before making their way back to their respective homes.

Up to this date, Kenos doesn't know how he and Uncle Nat survived that last encounter with the fighter. He was almost sure that something terrible was going to happen to them at the church. He knew that the freedom fighters had zero tolerance for disobedience. They often took swift actions even before they thought about the consequence. There was no way both men would have escaped the wrath of the fighter had it not being for the grace and mercy of the Almighty God.

CHAPTER TEN

Déjà Vu

BONG MINES SEEMED RELATIVELY calm even though a new rebel group had taken control of the city. There was not much information made available or given to the public by the management of BMC on potential or existing negotiations between them and the new rebel group. The new group seemed to have a small fighting force at least for the fighters that walked the streets of Bong Mines or compared to the first group of soldiers. Maybe this group was large in numbers, but they might have kept their forces from the eyes of the civilian population. However, they looked strategic in their planning and operations. The leader of the group would often visit the main bus stop located next to the train tracks, and residents would come around to listen to what he had to say. He would sing songs like, "The more we get together, the happier we shall be" as a prelude to beginning his talk with the community. He would sometimes dance, and lay out plans to curb crimes and dishonesty in the areas. At some of the meetings, he would periodically institute harsh disciples against anyone who they caught in crimes or considered enemy fighters. For the most part, the new group of militants was not too social. By this, I mean, they did not interact with the civilian population like the former fighters. However, they were instrumental in making sure that the management of BMC met the needs of the civilians. They opened the company's rice warehouse and distributed free rice and other food items to all who showed up at the distribution sites.

For months, Bong Mines remained peaceful and under control temporarily. The fear of another attack on the city was gradually fading away from the minds of Bong Miners. Residents began to come out of their homes and engage in their regular daily routines. Some of those who left town during the arrival of the new rebel group began to return to the city gradually. A few shops along the road from Nyien to Nyeablah opened for business while others remained closed. The local market opposite the train tracks opened partially but not on every day of the week. Most stores at the main bus stop remained closed probably because it was the main area where the leader of the new rebel group often visited. It appeared all was going well again in Bong Mines and life was beginning to return to some level of normalcy. The "Trio" managed to stay in the same area throughout the first attack on the city that repelled the first group of freedom fighters. There were times when Kerkula had to leave his two friends and go to Cephas Town to be with his younger brothers. His brothers had come to Bong Mines from the interior to stay for a while due to harassments and intimidations they were encountering in the village. Kerkula had to make sure that his brothers were safe and not in any trouble.

A Mere Coincidence

One early sunny afternoon, Kerkula had gone to take some food to his brothers in Cephas Town. They were out of food and had asked him to help them. While they were having a conversation in the living room of another uncle's house, a group of armed men on patrol from Nyeablah was walking through Cephas Town to Kiatokoota (Kia-to-koo-ta). They were walking to the main gate in Nyien. Kerkula opened the window to see who the men were. Accidentally, he came face-to-face with an old friend whom he grew up with in Gbarnga in the late 1980s. It was R.J.! He was dressed up in military uniform with a large weapon mounted across his chest. It appears the gun he was carrying was an automatic machine gun. As soon as R.J. spotted Kerkula, he winked and signaled him to come out and join them. He carefully but continuously kept on inviting Kerkula to come out and join the movement but did not want his commander or any other soldier to notice what he was doing. Kerkula became terrified and immediately shut the window. He had vowed to himself, his parents, and his entire family that he would never join the military or become a rebel fighter. All he wanted to do was to remain an ordinary civilian and a Christian. Carrying guns or using them was never his desire. Even though his father had one of the same firearms as a professional soldier defending his country, he knew it was not the will of God to take guns against another human being, no matter the reason or indifference.

It was the last time Kerkula would lay his eyes on his friend. It was on the same day that R.J. and his band of fighters left Bong Mines for Monrovia.

A JOURNEY TO BONG MINES

The new group of soldiers did not stay in Bong Mines for too long. They were in Bong Mines for less than a month. According to some Bong Miners who interacted with them more closely, the new fighters had a mission to go to Monrovia and not stay in Bong Mines. They were not interested in occupying any other city but Monrovia. They planned to capture a city, use it as a transit point and leave it for another town in their path toward Monrovia. The group had a history of maintaining and implementing such military strategy since it separated itself from the NPFL.

Return of the First Group

The departure of the new rebel group left Bong Mines vulnerable to any other militant group. Fortunately for some Bong Miners and at least for BMC management, the first group of freedom fighters who were repelled by the second group returned to Bong Mines in less than twenty-four hours after the departure of the second group was made public. However, their stay in Bong Mines wasn't for a long-anticipated period. Obviously, some Bong Miners had hoped that the return of the first group would have normalized the security situation, improve community living, and end all future attacks and counterattacks on the city. Regrettably, the return of the fighters did not bring a lasting solution or make a significant difference to the community as residents were anticipating. However, though the return of the fighters was short lived, there were negative and positive impacts on the community, especially on residents. There were some residents who were considered traitors or sympathizers of the second rebel group. Those residents suffered the consequence of being classified as traitors or sympathizers. Residents who were fortunate enough to anticipate what the impact of the return of the fighters would be fled the town early to save their lives. To this date, some of those residents who fled still sense the fear of being hunted, at least mentally and psychologically.

The next day, Kerkula rejoined his friends on John Hill where they lived. As usual, they visited Mamie, Kenos' girlfriend, in the marketplace to get their food supplies. They would take home what she gave them and prepare it as the only meal for the day. After cooking, they would sit around and eat, keep company, and later in the afternoon go to the church to attend choir practice, Bible studies, GAP meeting, or visit with friends in Bong Town. It was their daily routine, and the Trio followed it faithfully. Occasionally, they visited Kerkula's parents after his father, mother, and

140

other siblings safely arrived in Bong Mines. They would go and help his parents gather firewood and other essential food items. Upon Kerkula's father's arrival in Bong Mines, he spent a couple of months with his younger brother, Uncle Morris, before moving to his apartment in Camp Malonka (Ma-lon-ka). He had to move out because there was not enough room at this brother's home to accommodate his wife and the other children who had joined them a few months after they'd arrived.

Chilly Tuesday

It was on an early Tuesday morning, and the sun was beginning to rise. It felt a little chilly as the morning breeze from Mount Zaweah and Bong Peak swept across the city. A taste for spicy hot food was the desire of the Trio. Unlike other days, this time, they decided to visit the market early to get their food supplies and head home to cook. They wanted to cook soon because of the chilly weather. Moreover, they had planned to visit some friends in Bong Town during the evening hours. Before leaving the market, they invited Krubo to come over later so she could eat with them, but she declined their offer.

At home, the Trio prepared fried chicken greens with lots of hot red pepper and rice. The food was enough that they'd offer some of it to an elderly gentleman who lived next door and usually hung out with them to discuss politics and the Bible. The older man took the food which they had offered him and went to his bedroom and ate. He thanked the boys for providing his meal for the day and blessed them for being kind to him. They ate and talked all afternoon and later took naps in the living room. Soon, darkness fell, and the boys decided not to visit Bong Town as planned but stay at home since it was already late. So, each of them went to their respective bedrooms.

Kenos lived in the next building adjacent to the house in which Jake and Kerkula had their bedrooms. The house belonged to Jake's parents. His parents fled to Nimba County after the arrival of the first group of freedom fighters. Jake's room was in the main house, and Kerkula's in an annex at the back of the building. Kerkula's annex room was seated on a hill overlooking the houses down the streets and the roads below. The room had two windows; one of the windows faced the north end of town and the other the west end. He hardly opened the window to the north end because of the noise from the streets. He kept the window to the west opened during the day and at night to enjoy the midnight and early morning mountainous breeze which helped reduce the heat in his bedroom especially during the dry season. At night when the community or streets were quiet, Kerkula's room was a beautiful place to lay one's head and enjoy a good night sleep, but when the roads became busy, the noise and stomping of human feet became unbearable and frustrating. There was not much Kerkula could do about it because he needed a place to stay. He had to keep his window opened at night because there was no electricity and no fan to cool his room from the heat. The night breeze was the only source of natural cool air that went through his bedroom.

All Hell Breaks Loose

The night, for the most part, was peaceful and quiet. There were not many movements of vehicles or people in the streets. Usually at night, when darkness filled the earth, and everyone had gone to bed, one could easily hear cars driving through the streets and people talking as they walked by under Kerkula's window and on the roads beneath the hill. But on that night, it seemed as though people stopped moving and there were fewer vehicles in the streets. There were no indications that an attack on the city was imminent, neither had there been any announcement or rumors concerning any attack. The boys had gone to bed a little early that night. As usual, Kerkula left his bedroom window to the west side of town opened. They had eaten so much rice and greens that they slept heavily. At approximately 2:00 a.m. GMT, a loud explosion occurred somewhere between Nyeablah and Cephas Town. It was difficult to know if the explosion was a result of an enemy attack or something else. Up to date, the exact location of the explosion is not confirmed, but some believed that the first heavy weapon fired that night was done somewhere in that vicinity.

Red flames of fire splashed in the sky and the noise of the explosion woke Kerkula up immediately from his sleep. He left his bed and went to the window to see what was happening outside. Suddenly the sound of sporadic gunfire erupted, and there was screaming and yelling coming from everywhere. People began to run for their lives as the firing intensified. Some families left their homes leaving their kids behind while others stayed in bed. There were elderly folks who were trampled over trying to escape but couldn't move faster because the group began to increase in size. It became increasingly difficult to maneuver through the group into the camp

(Botota). More sounds of heavy gunfire followed as it quickly spread all over the west side of the city.

Kerkula knew firsthand based on his previous experiences not to get up and run with the crowd without first knowing who was doing the shootings, which directions they were coming from and which way was the safest route to take to avoid falling into danger. After a few minutes of assessment, he grabbed his wallet, put on his sneakers, his jacket, and his favorite baseball cap and walked out of his room. He ran up to Jake's bedroom, but he had already left. He attempted to go to find Kenos, but the shooting became heavy between the houses as though the fighting had already reached their community. He thought about going to Botota to find his uncle and his family, but it became difficult because there were movements of vehicles at high speed along the roads. He also thought about going to find his parents in Camp Malonka or his younger brother in Camp Benduma, but he quickly remembered what his father once told them to do in desperate situations when saving one's life at all cost became a necessity. He managed to make his way down the hill from his room onto the roads.

By this time, more and more people were fleeing Cephas Town, Kiatokoota, the train tracks area, and John Hill, respectively. It was now clear that the shootings were coming from the west of the city. He crossed the road leading down John Hill into Botota through a narrow opening in the wire fence and ran toward his uncle's house, but no one seemed to have been home. They had locked all the doors, cut off the lights and hid under the beds. With no one to let him into the house, he ran down the street toward his uncle's next-door neighbor's home closer to the swamp and onto the road which led to the main hospital. There he met Uncle Nat and two of the Lutheran youth members who had come from across the St. Paul River to bring him and his family some food and to visit with them.

He greeted them upon arrival at the place where they were standing and waiting to see which direction the fighters were going. The wait was not too long, and they began to run away together as the shooting quickly surrounded them. Stray bullets flew overhead, and some went into the swamp and onto the rooftop of the hospital. They ran as fast as they could and crossed the swamp into Bong Town close to Holy Cross. They decided to stop and see if the fighting was going to subside and not reach them but the more they delayed the closer the fight came.

"Déjà vu! Déjà vu! Déjà vu!" he whispered to himself as he looked in the eyes of Uncle Nat and the youth who were with them.

It dawned on him that it was happening all over again to him. Another walk was about to begin, unfortunately, this time unprepared and alone. He feared the worst for his younger brothers and his parents. He had no clue what was going to happen to them. He was not sure if they had stayed indoors like his uncle and family did or joined the fleeing crowd. He had hoped that they would flee into the bushes and find their way back to the interior where they would be more protected and safe. He worried about not having the opportunity to tell them what to say and do when they encountered a situation. He was hopeful that they would use the lessons learned from their time spent together during their walks from Harbel to Bong Mines. Time could only tell how effectively they would apply the lessons learned.

CHAPTER ELEVEN

Can't Stop Walking

THEY CONTINUED THEIR WALK through Bong Town going through the different communities and passing the homes of some residents they were familiar with and others whom they did not know. As they walked past the houses, they tried to encourage the residents to pack up and leave, but they paid them no mind. Some residents had already decided they were not leaving behind all that they had worked hard for over the years for looters to come and take it away. They would rather stay in their homes and die than run into the streets and be humiliated by strangers. Some had nowhere to go and had never left Bong Mines before. Bong Mines and its environs were all they have ever come to know. They believed leaving Bong Mines for an unknown city was exposing themselves to imminent dangers. The fear of the unknown made many residents of Bong Mines stay behind in their homes risking everything including their very lives and the lives of their beloved families.

The Last Man Standing

The last home Kerkula, Uncle Nat, and the other two youth members stopped at before finally leaving the city was the home of Mr. P. From all indications, Mr. P was the last senior staff of Bong Mines that Kerkula and Uncle Nat met face-to-face with before the city finally fell to the third group of rebel fighters. He was the last man standing. All the senior staff who resided within the community where they had passed seemed to have already left when Uncle Nat and Kerkula passed by. Both Kerkula and Uncle Nat went up to the house while the two youth members stayed down the road at the entrance to Mr. P's home to watch for movement of rebel fighters. Upon arrival at the

145

A JOURNEY TO BONG MINES

house, Mr. P was spotted wearing his pajamas with a pair of glasses on. He was reading a newspaper when he answered his front door.

"What are you boys doing here?" he asked Uncle Nat and Kerkula.

"We are trying to get out of Bong Mines, Mr. P," Uncle Nat replied.

"Where are you going?" Mr. P asked the boys.

"We are not sure, maybe somewhere further from here for a while until the fighting subsides," Uncle Nat responded.

"Well, I encourage you, boys, to go back home. Bong Mines will be fine. Nothing is going to happen. We are safe here," Mr. P said confidently.

"Mr. P, this is not an easy war. What we have seen already is nothing to joke about. This is very serious. We appeal to you to join us and leave this place," Uncle Nat petitioned Mr. P.

"I intend to stay here and so does my daughter. We are not leaving our home! Things will be fine! You boys go on if you have to go," Mr. P responded.

By this time, Kerkula managed to slip past Mr. P and went in the house to talk with Mr. P's daughter, who was standing at the window looking at Uncle Nat talking with her father. Like Uncle Nat, Kerkula tried to persuade Mr. P's daughter to get ready and leave Bong Mines but she was not sure of leaving without her father. She pleaded with Kerkula to join Uncle Nat in convincing her father for them to leave. While the talking was going on between Kerkula and Mr. P's daughter, he walked back into the living room and told her to take the "cookpot" out in the front yard and fill it up with charcoal because he wanted to heat some water to make himself tea to drink and to also take a bath.

Up in the hills, which were supposedly called "managers' hills," or where the managers live, especially the general manager, there was intense gunfire going on. Mr. P informed Uncle Nat and Kerkula that there was a standout resistance from a resident against the fighters. They did not know who put up the resistance and against what group of fighters. The Managers' hill was not too far from where Mr. P lived at the time of the incident. Hence, the sound of gunfire came much closer than expected. The echoes of bullets flying through the woods frightened and convinced Mr. P's daughter that there was a need to leave immediately. She hurriedly past her father, went into the house and put on some clothes, pretending as though she was feeling cold. She was now convinced about the nature and severity of the war as Uncle Nat had described, which was not to be taken for granted. Unfortunately, it did not change her father's mind about staying in Bong Mines. He went into his

CAN'T STOP WALKING

house and picked up a chair and came right back out and sat in it. As more and more people began to come running down the streets; some wounded, tired, scared, and others confused, the two youth posted at the entrance to Mr. P's home ran up the hill and cautioned both Uncle Nat and Kerkula that it was time to leave because things were getting worse.

With one last try, both Uncle Nat and Kerkula pleaded with Mr. P asking him to trust them and to come along to safety, but he insisted that he and his daughter were not leaving Bong Mines for another city. You could tell Mr. P's daughter did not want to stay behind. She tried to leave but feared the worst was about to come; she wouldn't leave her father alone, not for any reasons known to man. No words were convincing enough, no actions too terrifying, or no plans tempting enough to have persuaded her to leave her father behind. It was either they went together or stayed. She was willing to risk her young life and be with her father regardless of the outcome. It was evident that Mr. P and his daughter loved each other and were inseparable. There was nothing else that Uncle Nat and Kerkula could do to convince Mr. P or his daughter to leave.

At one point, it crossed Kerkula's mind to encourage Mr. P's daughter to leave with them secretly since she was young and still had a life ahead of her, but that would have been unfair to the old man. He wondered as he contemplated the idea of what would happen if she'd escaped leaving her father behind and the war never reached them, or her father lived through the war. How could she be able to see his face knowing that she abandoned him during troubled times? How could she be able to rekindle their excellent relationship? What could she tell her father was the reason for leaving him behind? What would have Mr. P thought about his wonderful daughter? Clueless to find answers to these and other questions going through his mind, he was forced to disregard his thoughts. Both men were forced to walk away hopelessly knowing they were leaving two beautiful individuals behind in harm's way. All that they had hoped for in convincing this family to go seemed to have shattered.

As they turned around and began to walk away toward the street, Kerkula's heart began to pound. He feared the worst was inevitable and bound to happen no matter what. He knew leaving Mr. P and his daughter behind could be the last time they'd see them. Remember, he had been through this experience before and knew precisely the activities of the fighters and what to expect. He could almost predict what was going to happen to those who refused to leave town. In his mind, he knew if Mr. P and his daughter would only allow themselves to come with them, they would have most likely saved their lives from the hands of the militants. Even though there were no guarantees of a happy end or a protected environment ahead of them, one could have only hoped that the adage "where there is life, there is hope" would have been their motivation to leave Bong Mines.

It only took one look as he turned around and saw her hands waved goodbye to them. He finally knew then; Mr. P and his beautiful and smart daughter were not leaving Bong Mines. Kerkula became emotional as he fought to hold back his tears. He did not want the other guys with him to see what he was going through. He'd hoped God could perform an instant miracle and change their minds to leave Bong Mines, but he did not. Maybe it was his will toward them or maybe something else. Only God will ever know why those two wonderful souls decided to stay behind. Mr. P's daughter was a good friend to him. They knew and had humble respect for each other. Though they were not close, they were good friends. He admired her eloquence and smartness as she did likewise to him.

Leaving the yard, they walked as fast as they could and joined a small group of people; almost the last group on the road from Bong Town. They passed by the previous set of houses onto a narrow pathway which led them into a grassy field leading to Dam 12. There were lots of people resting in the fields. There were people who had fled during the night and did not know where to go and others like Kerkula who had joined them as the fighting progressed. Some if not most of them were hoping that the outbreak of hostility may not have lasted too long, and they would have been able to return to their respective homes. Unfortunately, the more they stuck around, the worse conditions became. There were a few people who managed to escape during broad daylight who informed those waiting in the open fields that returning to Bong Mines was unsafe and the silliest decision anyone was willing to take.

There were babies with their mothers, older folks, and young boys and girls as well. Two gentlemen appeared from the narrow path ahead of the crowd wearing bloody clothes. They claimed they had been shot and were seeking help, but no one had medications to help them. Those among the group who had technical skills in medicine or nursing assisted them by tying their wound with pieces of cloths to suppress the bleeding, but that was all they could do to help. Further along the grassy roads, three young kids were sitting in the grass crying frantically. It seemed their parents must have abandoned them or got caught up in some situation. No one was there to care for them. They had three dollars and fifteen cents with them along with a handful of dried cornmeal (aka co-co-do-lo). One of the three kids was a three-month-old baby. A few yards from where the kids were sitting was another little girl who was sitting alone with no one next to her. As the group began to move forward, Uncle Nat decided that they take the three kids along with them to a safe place rather than leave them in the grass to die. They picked up the three kids and began to walk away, suddenly the little girl sitting alone cried out, "Uncle, please don't leave me behind, I want to come with you too." Kerkula picked her up and handed her to one of the youths who was going with them since he already had another kid on his shoulders.

No Turning Back

It was dawn, and the sun began to rise above the northern horizon. The heat wave was also increasing quickly. They found themselves in an open terrain with no place to hide or seek shelter. They had to make quick decisions about which way to go. Some in the crowd suggested going back to Bong Mines. Others said to stay in the vicinity for a couple more hours to see if conditions in Bong Mines would improve, then they could return during the night when no one could quickly notice them. There were also others who decided it was not worth taking the risk of returning to Bong Mines or staying in the open fields. Besides, those who came during daylight had already warned the group from going back to Bong Mines. So, they decided to begin the journey out of the area. Uncle Nat, Kerkula, and the two youth carried the kids on their shoulders from Dam 12 as far as a small village in the town of Wheyala (Wee-ya-la). They decided to leave the three-month-old baby with a woman who accepted to breastfeed and take care of her. The baby was becoming weaker and seemed hungry, but there was no food for her to eat. Therefore, they decided to leave her in a secure place to save her life.

They immediately got back on the road knowing they still had a long way to go. They were not sure how to get there because they did not understand the terrain. They made another quick decision on going directly to Salala instead of traveling a bush path since it was on the main road and there were more displaced people walking the same route as well. They knew walking together in groups on an open road was the safest thing to do even though it sometimes proved the contrary. They reached

Salala during the late afternoon hours. There, they met a friend to Uncle Nat. His name was Rev. Gbono. He was a pastor of the Lutheran Church in Salala. He accepted to take and care for the other three kids so that Uncle Nat, Kerkula, and the others would be relieved of carrying the kids on their shoulders since they still had a long way to go. Rev. Gbono was familiar with Salala and understood the routes in and out of the city. He directed Uncle Nat to go by way of Gboquenima (Gbo-que-ni-ma) and instructed him to ask anyone in the town for directions to his hometown in Kokoyah (Ko-ko-yah).

Uncle Nat thanked Rev. Gbono for giving them directions and his willingness to take care of the kids. He promised to stay in touch with them. It was the last time they saw Rev. Gbono or the kids. They bade the Reverend goodbye and started their walk once again toward Kokoyah. On one occasion after several years, Uncle Nat informed Kerkula through a telephone conversation that he contacted one of the kids and she is grown up and doing well in life. He plans to visit her at their home in Salala. There is no record of Rev. Gbono's whereabouts. However, Uncle Nat believed Rev. Gbono took loving care of the kids, survived the war, and is doing fine somewhere in Liberia.

The Road Ahead

The evening was approaching slowly but surely, and they still had more miles to cover. Each one of them seemed tired. They had not eaten any cooked food since they left Bong Mines. They had pretty much survived on sugar cane, mangoes, oranges, and other fruits they found along the roads. Walking faster was not an option for them, even though it was getting late. All they had hoped for was to make it to the next town and leave the main roads. By this time, some of the displaced people who had started the walk with them from Bong Mines were either gone ahead or branched out onto other roads that led to different villages along the way. However, due to the walking distance ahead, others may have fallen behind or gone back to the open fields with the hope of making it back to Bong Mines.

They finally reached Gboquenima (Gbo-que-ni-ma) which was the next big town along the road followed by Gbatala (Gba-ta-la). Upon arrival in Gboquenima, they were ordered to go through a security checkpoint for inspection. During the examination, one of the freedom fighters who claimed he was a G2—an intelligent office—was kind enough to give the directions for Kokoyah to Uncle Nat. He showed them how to get there quickly by way of a bush path. He told Uncle Nat and the others not to go by way of Gbatala if they were going to Kokoyah. He warned them of the possibility of conscription. He offered to draw a map listing all the towns along the narrow paths to Kokoyah and illustrated precisely how to get through to each one of them. He was a kind gentleman, his help with the directions made a significant difference in relaxing their minds as they traveled through the bushes.

One thing that amazed Kerkula about the fighter's interactions with them was his idiosyncrasy. He kept a smile on his face throughout the interactions. He talked a lot and often praised himself as though he was perfect or had never done any wrong. He used words loosely as though he did not know and value the true meaning of them.

After he completed the drawing of the map, he handed it to Uncle Nat and said, "Go down this little road behind that house," pointing his finger at a small white house on a hill, "and you will be in Kokoyah. This road will lead you to the next town called Conola [Co-no-la], which is not far from where you are going," the fighter added. His sense of direction and description of the routes to Kokoyah made everyone feel at ease and believe Kokoyah was few steps away.

Everyone except Uncle Nat was happy for the excellent news the fighter had given to them. They were excited that they would finally be home within an abbreviated time after being on the roads for so long without food and clean drinking water. Kerkula noticed Uncle Nat was smiling after the fighter made his comment. He was not sure why he was smiling but was interested in knowing. He later found out that the soldier was from the Bassa ethnic tribe and grew up within the area. There is a joke about the Bassa tribe, especially those from Kokoyah. Some Liberians believe when a Bassa man or woman gives you a direction to a place like the one provided by the fighter and says, "The place is not far away, or it is right over there," you should be prepared to walk hours or even a whole day. Some also believed that the Bassa tribe does not associate walking long distances with time. It is not that they do not have regard for the importance of time when walking long distances; they do not consider it a factor. It is believed that walking long miles on foot is a genetic trait given to them by their ancestors.

It was the last time in many years that Uncle Nat and the others would see, come closer to a highway, or walk a busy road again. They followed the hand-sketched map the fighter had given them and maneuvered their way

151

A JOURNEY TO BONG MINES

through the bushes as they journeyed several hours from one village to the next. It was the beginning of the second phase of their walk with the hope of reaching his hometown in Kokoyah, Bong County.

Up to this day, it puts smiles on Kerkula's face whenever he thinks about what the fighter said to them about Kokoyah being right behind the house as though it was a reality. Indeed, we are all the same but uniquely different. We see, understand, and value things differently as bequeathed or bestowed unto us by our creator.

APPENDIX

*A Glossary of Traditional Liberian
Names and Meanings*

Names of Cities and Towns

Gbarnga   on the farm (some believe it means a small pile of dead branches or wood)

Totota   town named after the former chief, Kwemleh Toto, and his family

Salala   name of a body of water

Gbatala   at a body of water called Gba

Kakata   name of a person

Mawah   wash it or wash on it

Haindii   home of a former Paramount chief

Nyian   in the sand

Nyeablah   split hill or between the hills

Zaweata   Bassa name for a mountain

Suakoko   name of a former powerful town chief, Nai Suah

Gboquenima   the door on the rock or behind the rock

Loguatuo   a town on a hill called Logua

Kokoyah/Klo-Klo-ya   (a solid or firm object or substance)—a district in upper Bong County mostly inhabited by the Kpelle, Mano, Gio, and predominately Bassa tribes.

APPENDIX

Smell-No-Taste	a supposedly made-up name given to a town in Liberia based on the way of life of the early inhabitants (Bassa tribe)

Names of Individuals

Kerkula	a traditional Kpelle name
Sieneh	a traditional Via/Mandingo name
Makenneh	a traditional Via, Gola, and Mandingo name
Freedom fighters	a person who takes part in a violent struggle to achieve a political goal especially to overthrow their government
Rebels	a person who rises in opposition or armed resistance against an established government or ruler

Names of Objects

Mount Zaweah	Bassa name for this mountain
Bong Peak	a name given to the second mountain
Liberty Bill	local Liberian currency
Bamboo Tree	bamboos are a group of woody perennial evergreen plants in the true grass family Poaceae—it is used by locals to make furniture and furniture-like items

Names of Tribes and Terms

Kru	found on the West Coast of Liberia (Grand Kru County), they are mainly involved in fishery and trade
Grebo	subgroup of the Kru, mainly found in the southeastern coast Maryland and Grand Kru Counties
Via	mostly found in Grand Cape Mount County, they are known for their indigenous syllabic writing system
Mende	producers of woven textiles and from Montserrado County, western Liberia

APPENDIX

Kpelle	the largest ethnic group in Liberia, they are from Bong County
Mandingo	mostly Muslims who engage in trade and commerce; found relatively in all counties in Liberia but predominantly in Nimba County
Bassa	once known as "people of the forest," good hunters of animals and gatherers of fruits and vegetables, they live in Grand Bassa County, southeastern Liberia
Mano	mostly found in the northeastern part of Liberia in Nimba County; excellent in art and craft and good musicians and farmers
Krahn	mostly found in the northeastern part of Liberia; originally, they were farmers, hunters, and fishermen
Gio	tribal group in northeastern Liberia and the Ivory Coast, they are from Nimba County
San-ga-lay-go-wa	you come against us and fail; we come against you and win
Single file	a line of people or things arranged one behind another

Name of Food Products and Drinks

Okra	tropical food
Bitter balls	tropical food
Pepper	tropical food
Kittely	tropical food
Palm wine / Bamboo wine	locally produced alcoholic beverage made from palm trees and sold in the local markets, it is usually consumed by the locals, especially men

BIBLIOGRAPHY

Bellamy, C. "Children Are War's Greatest Victims." *OECD Observer*, May 22, 2002. http://oecdobserver.org/news/archivestory.php/aid/701/Children_are_wars_greatest_victims.html.

Bennett, W. J. *The Moral Compass: Stories for a Life's Journey*. New York: Simon & Schuster, 1995.

Cabral, J. P. S. "Water Microbiology. Bacterial Pathogens and Water." *International Journal of Environmental Research and Public Health*. 7 (2010) 365–70. https://www.ncbi.nlm.nih.gov/pmc/articles/PMC2996186.

Dodo, L. "Firestone Liberia to Lay Off 800 Employees." *Front Page Africa*, March 18, 2019. https://frontpageafricaonline.com/news/firestone-liberia-to-lay-off-800-employees.

Duddu, P. "Top Ten Fastest Trains in the World." *Railway Technology*, August 28, 2013. https://www.railway-technology.com/features/feature-top-ten-fastest-trains-in-the-world.

Firestone Natural Rubber Company. "Liberian Civil War." Firestone Liberia website, June 22, 2014. https://www.firestonenaturalrubber.com/our-positions/liberian-civil-war.

Ghanaian Chronicle. "Rebel Groups in Africa, How Are They Funded?" *Modern Ghana*, January 15, 2013. https://www.modernghana.com/news/439652/rebel-groups-in-africa-how-are-they-funded.html.

Huntsman, J. M. *Winners Play by the Rules: Keep Your Moral Compass*. Upper Saddle River, NJ: Pearson Prentice-Hall, 2010.

Ishida, M. "Rebuttal to Claimed Refutations of Duncan MacDougall's Experiment on Human Weight Change at the Moment of Death." *Journal of Scientific Exploration* 24 (2010) 5–39.

Kau, Y. M. *The People's Liberation Army and China's Nation-Building*. White Plains, NY: International Arts and Sciences Press, 1973.

Kerkar, R. "Health Benefits of Sugarcane Juice & Its Nutritional Facts, Side Effects." ePainAssist.com, January 4, 2019. https://www.epainassist.com/diet-and-nutrition/health-benefits-of-sugarcane-juice.

Kottayam, Aravindan. "Recovery in Rubber Prices Unlikely in 2019 Due to Unfavorable Demand-Supply Fundamentals." *Hindu BusinessLine*, January 4, 2019. https://www.thehindubusinessline.com/economy/agri-business/recovery-in-rubber-prices-unlikely-in-2019-due-to-unfavourable-demand-supply-fundamentals/article25913469.ece.

Kraaij, F. P. M. van der. *Liberia: Past & Present of Africa's Oldest Republic*. Website. Created March 26, 2018. http://www.liberiapastandpresent.org.

BIBLIOGRAPHY

MacDougall, D. "Hypothesis concerning Soul Substance Together with Experimental Evidence of the Existence of Such Substance." *Journal of the American Medical Association* 4 (1907) 240–43.

Ministry of Foreign Affairs. "His Excellency T. Ernest Eastman Is Dead." Government of the Republic of Liberia, Ministry of Foreign Affairs, February 28, 2011. http://www.mofa.gov.lr/public2/2press.php?news_id=331&related=7&pg=sp.

Moore, C., and F. Gino. "Ethically Adrift: How Others Pull Our Moral Compass from True North, and How We Can Fix It." June 17, 2013. https://dash.harvard.edu/handle/1/10996801.

The Observatory of Economic Complexity. https://atlas.media.mit.edu.

Paye-Layleh, J. "Firestone in Liberia Pursues Drastic Layoffs, Worrying Many." *Washington Times*, March 29, 2019. https://www.washingtontimes.com/news/2019/mar/29/firestone-in-liberia-pursues-drastic-layoffs-worry/.

Sample, I. "Is There Lightness after Death?" *Guardian*, February 19, 2004. https://www.theguardian.com/film/2004/feb/19/science.science.

Schlein, L. "UNICEF Says Children Are Main Victims of War." VOANews.com, September 23, 2014. https://www.voanews.com/a/unicef-says-children-main-victims-of-war/2459908.html.

Shapiro, E., and D. Shapiro. "Overcoming F.E.A.R.: False Evidence Appearing Real." Oprah.com, April 30, 2010. http://www.oprah.com/spirit/transform-your-fear-into-courage/all.

"Smell-No-Taste." Geoview.info. http://lr.geoview.info.

Thomas, K. "How Liberia's Ebola Outbreak Led to Water Access Reform." *Pacific Standard*, December 10, 2018. https://psmag.com/social-justice/liberia-works-to-improve-its-water-system.

Tzu, S. *The Art of War*. New York: Penguin, 2009.

UNICEF. "Report on the Impact of Armed Conflict on Children." August 26, 1996. https://www.unicef.org/graca/a51-306_en.pdf.

United Nations Economic Commission for Africa (UNECA). "Africa's Health and Financing: Pathways to Growth and Prosperity." GBCHealth, September 27, 2018. http://www.gbchealth.org/news-un-high-level-dialogue-africas-health-finance-pathways-to-economic-growth-prosperity.

United States Environmental Protection Agency. "Quick Guide for Disinfectant Products for Drinking Water Use by Public Water Systems." EPA, September 2017. https://www.epa.gov/sites/production/files/2017-09/documents/quick_guide_for_disinfectant_products_for_drinking_water_use.pdf.

Webmaster Admin. "Great Opportunity for Liberian Poultry Farmers." *Daily Observer*, May 16, 2014. https://www.liberianobserver.com/opinion/editorials/great-opportunity-for-liberian-poultry-farmers/.

Wilson, S. T. K., et al. "The Mining Sector of Liberia: Current Practices and Environmental Challenges." *Environmental Science Pollution Research* 24 (2017) 18711–20. doi.org/10.1007/s11356-017-9647-4.

World Health Organization (WHO). "The Abuja Declaration: Ten Years On." August 2011. https://www.who.int/healthsystems/publications/abuja_declaration/en.

———. "Drinking-Water." Fact sheet. February 7, 2018. https://www.who.int/newsroom/fact-sheets/detail/drinking-water.